KEEP
STEPPING

A step-by-step journey

to a better view of mental illness

By

Mike Owen

For all those that have influenced my life, my faith, and my future.

CONTENTS

Acknowledgments

Thanks to Kay, my family, and friends for their love and support during my challenges and recovery.

Thanks to those Facebook friends who I've yet to meet, but because they "get it", I feel like I've known for years.

Thanks to everyone who supported me, pushed me, cajoled me, cared for me, loved me, and got me back to where I should be.

Thanks to Coco for keeping me going, for walking alongside me and, even though she's been mistreated in the past, for showing a love that can't be surpassed. Who rescued who?

Preface

I believe that we all have unwritten books inside of us.

Some are short stories, some war and peace.

Some are fast paced, others slow burners.

Some are hard to swallow, others are easier to take.

Some have happy beginnings, middles, and ends.

Some have difficult starts and happy ever afters.

Some have joyful introductions and traumatic finales.

Some are full of mystery, others easier to solve.

Some are factual, some fiction, some fake.

Some are difficult to open, others easily shared.

Some are crumpled, torn and weathered.

Some pristine, protected and uneventful.

Some are kept under wraps, others free to view.

All are unique, individual, and contain personal battles.

None can be compared yet so much can be gleaned from the experiences within their bindings.

Share kindly, study carefully, digest well.

Author's Note

I always thought there was a book inside me but never in my life thought it would be a book about a battle with mental health.

For most of my life, I've been able to deal with any stress or pressure that occurred, either at work or at home.

I had a fantastic childhood. A great family. Two amazing parents. A great brother and good friends. Relatively secure, well-paid job. Nice, affordable home. Low amounts of debt. A solid faith. Strong will. Brilliantly supportive wife. Two incredible children. Enjoyable social life. Fulfilling volunteer youth work. No concerns about mental health.

The only blot on my landscape was my heart and its two congenital heart defects. One was diagnosed at my first yearly health check and repaired when I was seven. The other I controlled for thirty-eight years, using a medically recommended breathing technique, until it was diagnosed and destroyed in 2004.

Given the two defects, my heart has always been my Achilles Heel. Viruses, fatigue, and over exercise would always induce a severe bout of palpitations that I would manage to control with the breathing technique. But in 2013, I developed palpitations that couldn't be controlled, and this started my battle with mental health.

A battle that turned into a war, with distinct, difficult conflicts, sometimes debilitating, sometimes dangerous, sometimes damaging, sometimes invigorating, sometimes enlightening, and many with the potential to hamper or even destroy my progress.

During my recovery, as I fought each battle, and after sharing experiences with fellow mental health sufferers, I've realised that every mental health battle is different. Each unique to the individual person. Different background. Different duration. Different cause. Different triggers. Different symptoms. Different severity. Different recovery techniques. Different recovery times. Different outcomes.

This is my ride on a random roller coaster that defied gravity, overlooked G-Force, had blind corners, unseen drops, very dark passages, blinding lights, and gaping gaps, that I hoped would be filled in time. And then there's the flat, calm, tranquil drifts that I just wanted to continue and continue, while being forever on alert for the next unexpected drop.

This is the story of my battle, my numerous battles, this is the story of my war on mental health.

My story from survival and an unexpected diagnosis through misunderstandings, support challenges, cardiological relief, zero confidence, despair, cage-rattling, counselling, track-covering, and guilt-tripping to forgiveness, stability, renewed fitness, and peace via difficulties reconnecting, celebrating, balancing, educating, liberating, and, finally, closure.

"Reflect your light all around you, so everyone may see.

When the blind sneer from an obtuse angle, refraction is the key."

"The power to change direction, while not dimming your beam, may just change everything."

Survival

I don't remember a great deal about my early years. I think the open-heart operation in 1973, when I was 7 years of age, robbed me of those memories.

After speaking to my parents in 2017, I discovered that my congenital heart defect was discovered by the District Nurse at my first annual check-up. At my cardiology appointment in 2017, my cardiologist informed me that the heart defect was a large Atrial Septum Defect (ASD). The wall that forms after birth to split the top heart chamber into two hadn't developed completely.

Given the symptoms after the heart surgery in 1973, I can only assume that the symptoms in my earlier years were worse. To use a British Heart Foundation slogan, it was a "fight for every heartbeat" from the day I was born.

Although the heart operation was successful; given the equipment, technology, and techniques in use in the early 1970s, the invasive surgery left scar tissue on my heart. I found out in 2004 that the scar tissue can generate its own heartbeat, further complicating my heart's stability.

Between the ages of 7 and 38, I continually struggled with long bouts of palpitations, usually after exercise or when I was struck down with a virus. The palpitations produced very strong and fast but regular beats that could last for hours or days. Until the age of 21, I had no way of controlling these palpitations, I just had to sit them out and wait for my heart to return to its normal beat.

Soon after I turned 21, my care was transferred from Myrtle Street Children's Hospital in Liverpool to Southport Hospital under the consultancy of Dr Serlin. He demonstrated a breathing technique called the Valsalva Manoeuvre which I could use to reset my heart rate from over 200 beats a minute to 60 beats a minute within half a second. This breathing technique revolutionised my life, enabling me to be more active, even if it meant my heart would go fast, because I knew that I could reset my heartbeat in an instant.

Even though I had this weapon in my armoury, I was still wary about overexerting myself. I avoided physical contact while playing football or kept to low levels when walking but at least I could live my life without spending hours recovering.

It was a different story when viruses struck as, in many cases, the Valsalva Manoeuvre didn't work, and I had to resort to waiting for my heart rate to reduce over time. I could guarantee that at least twice a year a virus would take over my body, raise my heartbeat, I'd be confined to bed for three or four days and then take a similar amount of time to start to regain my strength.

In June 2004, my heart started going fast without warning, even when I was doing the most basic of things, like walking upstairs or bending down too quickly. I would use the Valsalva Manoeuvre multiple times a day and as soon as I'd controlled my heartbeat, it would go fast again.

I decided that I would wait to see if the palpitations were the early warning sign of a virus but even though the palpitations continued, there were no symptoms to explain this deterioration.

Even though my heart was struggling, I could still function. Instead of being confined to bed, my heart would be ok during the week, allowing me to continue to work, and the attacks would occur at the weekend, when I was more physically active.

At the end of July, I was finally struck down with a virus and after a few days in bed I felt well enough to return to work. However, after I had finished my morning shower, my heart started to race. This time, even the Valsalva Manoeuvre didn't help, and I ended up driving to my

GP with my heart pounding away at over 200 beats per minute.

The GP took one look at me and told me to get to Hospital as soon as possible. This would be the first of three visits to A & E in a four-week period.

Each time, the doctors would try various methods to reset my heart but, in the end, the only way that worked was with a drug called Amiodarone which, when given intravenously, would slowly, over a period of hours, bring my heart back to a more natural rhythm.

It was during my last stay in A & E that I was given a diagnosis that initially shook my world.

One of the doctors had spotted a small irregular impulse on my ECG trace. A tiny, indicative Delta Wave that exposed the cause of years of palpitations and I was diagnosed with Wolff-Parkinson-White syndrome.

The syndrome is caused by an extra connection in my heart's electrical system which, when active, would send my heartbeat into chaos and induce a type of palpitation called Supra Ventricular Tachycardia (SVT), a very fast, very strong, but very regular beat.

At first, I was mortified at the diagnosis but then it transpired that there was the chance for a complete cure.

By ablating the additional pathway, using keyhole surgery to locate and destroy the extra connection, there was a 95% chance of the SVT episodes being stopped for good.

In October 2004, I had a successful ablation and after a few weeks of convalescing, I was back at work, SVT free, and able to really start to rebuild my shattered confidence.

Within months I was playing football without any issues. My game became more physical. I could walk for miles up inclines that I would never have dreamt of attempting before the ablation. I became stronger. For the first time in my life my heart was very quiet, very regular, and very stable.

I could take on more challenging tasks at work. I could deal with the stress and anxiety with ease and that increased my standing within the department.

And then the departmental structure changed. I became more isolated. Worked on complex, old, draining and business-critical tasks with little or no experienced peer support. I felt out of my depth, exposed, and this increased the stress levels dramatically.

In 2012, I was off work for six weeks with stress.

And then in 2013, for the first time in seven years, my heart started to palpitate again, but this type of palpitation was different to the SVT episodes that I'd experienced before. The beats were faster, more erratic, quieter, and totally disabling.

Over the next six years the palpitations would occur time and time again.

As the palpitations were different, I didn't feel confident enough to use the Valsalva Manoeuvre that had proved beneficial before so, again, I just had to ride them out.

I saw a cardiologist in 2014 and although, on the ECG, my heart appeared ok and he was happy that there were no major issues with my heart, the palpitations kept on being triggered.

Eventually, through dietary changes and moderate levels of exercise, I managed to reduce the frequency of the attacks but in 2017, when my anxiety levels shot up, I fell into complete despair and, because I had started to feel better, I thought that I would never recover.

Apart from a few years, directly after my ablation, every year had been a battle with my heart issues. Sometimes I'd come very close to either dying or being disabled by either a stroke or seizure.

At times, I wasn't living but only surviving.

"That moment when it starts to dawn on you that you are feeling less of the person you were forced to be and fought against becoming and more the person you used to be and that you don't need to fight anymore!"

"If you see or experience something that you feel needs to change then don't walk away.

Stand up, speak out, touch nerves, rattle cages, ruffle feathers, throw cats into pigeons and make waves!"

Downtime

My stress levels started to increase in 2010, soon after the team structures changed, and continued to escalate through 2011 and 2012. From when my heart first reacted to the long-lasting effects of stress, in August 2013, until I regained confidence in my heart, in October 2019, the episodes of palpitations varied in length, severity, and frequency.

At their height in April 2014, the episodes were very intense, feeling like five different heartbeats, protracted and very scary. After my experiences of hospital visits in 2004, I kept giving my heart an extra five minutes to reset itself but after 36 hours I had almost given up hope. I was ready to throw in the towel. I never had suicidal thoughts but at that moment I told my heart to do its worst. Soon after, by some miracle, my heart returned to its normal beat.

Another shorter fifteen-hour bout followed in May 2014.

Even though those two episodes were very disabling, the effects of waking up in the middle of the night with my heartbeat out of sync or very short bursts of palpitations had the same effect of increasing the anxiety and further exacerbating the challenges with my heart.

Over time, I became totally preoccupied by my heartbeat.

Every waking hour, every piece of exercise, every item of food, every drink, and every task at work, I'd be checking my heart. Listening and monitoring, tensely waiting for the next ectopic (extra) beat that could either result in a small flutter or escalate into hours of debilitating palpitations.

The preoccupation affected my confidence, my concentration, my motivation, my speech, my ability to do even the simplest of tasks, what I could eat, what I could drink, where I could walk, what I could do and, most importantly, my inner self.

In 2015, things really started to get on top of me. As well as dealing with the anxiety-driven heart problems, other factors were bombarding me from several sides. This is when I felt at my lowest, after five years of struggle, I couldn't take any more. I wanted peace and all I had was turmoil and not just in my heart but my whole life and psyche.

I reached out and thankfully my wife was there for me. I'm not sure where I would have ended up if she hadn't responded.

That support allowed me to take stock of my situation. I made decisions that would allow me to regain a semblance of control. I felt I'd turned a corner, but it would be another two and half years until I would really start to recover.

I decided to take my foot off the pedal at work, to not let the work-related stress and pressure ruin the summer of 2015, as it had done for the previous five summers.

The decision followed the sad news of the untimely deaths of two young men that I'd known through Boys' Brigade. Those tragic losses demonstrated to me how preciously short and precariously fragile life really is and I was extremely thankful to be able to look forward to another summer.

I wanted to get back to the level of fitness that I last enjoyed in 2009, five years after my life-changing ablation.

The steps I took started to take effect. The frequency of the palpitations reduced, as did their severity, but they still occurred when I did too much or had to deal with stressful situations.

I'd removed a lot of the triggers that I thought were causing the episodes. The caffeine. The alcohol. I tried to reduce the stress and increase my exercise levels.

At the start of 2017, I started to feel more peace and stability. My confidence started to grow and that allowed my fitness to improve which in turn increased my confidence further.

But in May 2017, when the news was full of terrorist attacks and disasters, the despondency returned.

The terror attacks had a profound effect on me.

For years, I'd been following the events in Syria with unnatural preoccupation. The fear I felt of escalation and the conflict spreading further afield filled me with dread. I could see nothing but doom and gloom. The terror attacks in London and Manchester brought the situation very close to home. I was terrified with the reaction that the attacks may have caused and the tit for tat retaliation that I expected would have resulted.

All the work I had done to get myself back on track was lost. I wasn't just back at square one but, as I had a felt better for a few months, I was in a much worse position. When I was pushed back into that dark hole it was deeper, darker, scarier and more depressing.

I felt lost. I'd tried everything to improve my situation and seen a glimpse of a recovery but ended up in back in despair. The feelings of 2015 returned with a vengeance. I didn't know which way to turn.

As in April 2014, when my heart miraculously returned to sinus rhythm out of the blue, I needed another heavenly intervention to rescue me again. In 1973 and 2004, when I required the help from other people who appeared in my life at the right time, I could only hope that I would be put in a similar position again.

"Fear and paranoia have been replaced by reality and control,
Vigilance by obliviousness,
Noise by silence,
And false dawns by new hope."

"A new broom can only sweep clean, if it's allowed to see what's been previously swept under the carpet!"

Recognition

Following the flare up of palpitations that started in August 2013, and to reduce the possibility of being "stranded" at work thirty miles from home, I resorted to working from home so I could continue to support the projects that I had implemented in recent months.

Unfortunately, as the team sizes had reduced, there was insufficient, experienced resource to deal with any problems that occurred and because of this I felt incredible pressure to keep on working even though, with hindsight, I should have taken time off sick.

My workload through 2013, 2014, and 2015, did not relent and I continued to work from home on many occasions, sometimes for a couple of days before I felt more settled, other times I would work from home for weeks. During those three years, I only took time off sick when I was confined to bed, for example, when I was subjected to the two lengthy bouts of palpitations in 2014.

In July 2014, shortly before the implementation of another major project, I woke up at 5.30 a.m. with my heart beating very erratically. To try and settle, and so I didn't wake my wife, I lay on the sofa and decided to text work to try and rescope the implementation schedule and reduce the pressure on my shoulders.

Work's response was that I should ensure that there was sufficient documentation to enable another member of staff to pick up my work, if I wasn't able to complete the implementation.

Things changed when my anxiety flared up in May 2017.

Again, I ended up working from home or, as the project work had subsided, I was able to take time off sick without feeling like I was letting my team down. I was signed off by my GP for couple of weeks.

On the 27th of June, I attended a "Welfare Check" at work. The meeting seemed very clinical.

During the meeting I was handed a leaflet for a free telephone counselling service and I was told to contact them and arrange counselling for myself. This filled me with dread. I had always struggled to speak to people on the phone, and the thought of having to explain my situation to a stranger over the phone made my anxiety increase even further.

An appointment was made with me to see the company doctor to discuss my fitness for work. The appointment was at his surgery in Whalley on the 4th of July. I'd never heard of the company doctor and thought he may be a new initiative that the company had embarked on. I found out later, from a close friend who used to work with me, that she had visited the company doctor in 2008.

This revelation made me wonder why I hadn't been referred to the company doctor in 2012, when I had been off sick with stress for six weeks. Why hadn't my fitness to work been checked then?

All I could assume was that the company doctor would have reduced my hours or recommend my workload was reduced, putting the projects planned for 2013 and 2014 at risk, due to the lack of experience in the system areas affected.

So, what was different in 2017? Why was the company doctor now an option?

Maybe it was because my workload allowed it and that the cause of my flare up in 2017 was due to external factors.

It was time to recognise my struggles and take action.

"We watch our diet, measure our exercise and monitor our sleep but do we mind our mind?"

"Treat your mind well, it has the power to destroy and to restore! Choose wisely!"

"When someone finally shines a light on their poor handling of your past, use it to illuminate their failings rather than cast a shadow on your successes."

Diagnosis

As I made my way to the company doctor's surgery in Whalley, I was feeling more settled but still very nervous about what to expect and how he would view my situation.

I expected him to be biased towards the company that he represented, so outwardly I tried to ensure that I was holding things together, to give the impression that I was ok to return to work.

I entered Doctor Andrews' room full of trepidation.

The conversation started off quite dryly and, as I expected, we discussed how I was feeling at the time and how I'd been feeling over the previous few weeks.

The consultation moved naturally on to my cardiac history and I shared my experiences of the previous seven years, outlining the challenges I had faced. Working in isolation, on old, fragile systems, with minimal peer-level support, out of my depth, and in unfamiliar environments.

Then as the appointment ended, Doctor Andrews uttered a sentence that would change my life -

"I'm concerned about your mental resilience and your psychological vulnerability."

My immediate reaction to his concerns was to deny that it was possible. I'd never had mental health problems – my situations were always physical. I was in shock.

The meeting ended and during the drive back home, the sentence kept circling round my head. I couldn't understand how it was possible for me to be struggling mentally. I wasn't weird. I wasn't strange. I wasn't mental.

Ironically, as I drove round a roundabout, I realised that it was what I needed to hear, even though it was very difficult to reconcile.

In the same way as when I learnt that I had Wolff-Parkinson-White syndrome, when a nurse told me with an off-the-cuff remark while she was giving me my medicine, Doctor Andrews' unexpected sentence would be instrumental in my recovery from the mental illness that he had spotted behind the mask that I was wearing.

Now that I had been heard, I could start to heal.

Doctor Andrews had recognised that the concerns about my heart were fuelling my anxiety which then increased my cardiological fears.

He recommended that I have a fresh cardiology check-up, to hopefully reassure my worries about my heart and then attend sessions of Cognitive Behavioural Therapy to address the anxiety.

He would write a letter to work and send a copy to me for my records.

After a few weeks, his letter arrived at home. Before I opened it, I was worried about what he had included in the letter.

Would he cover everything I'd said about the previous seven years or would he overlook that in favour of work?

Would he mention his concerns about my poor mental health?

What would his recommendations include?

I can remember the total relief as I read the letter. It was so encouraging to finally have someone's support and understanding.

I had all the impetus I needed to start to take things forward.

"Spontaneity has the power to lift someone
out of the blue!"

"Master the art of surprising yourself
it's not as crazy as it sounds!"

"If they make you feel bad, ignore them.
If they make you feel good, embrace them."

July 2017

Coping Mechanisms

16th July 2017

Yesterday, I met someone who I've never met before and will probably never meet again.

A group from Rochdale, a place close to my heart, were visiting our church for their annual away day. I was there, during my walk with my dog, Coco, to set up the audio/visual equipment for their use during the day.

After they'd settled in, I left to walk home but Coco wanted to get a lift with her Grandad (my dad) who was just setting off in his car.

As Coco was digging her heels in, a man from the group came over to talk to her. I explained that she was nervous and that it wasn't a good idea to get too close due to her issues from before she was rescued.

The man said, "Dogs never forget do they and, unlike us, they don't have coping mechanisms."

He then went on to tell me that, due to his active service in Northern Ireland and as a prison officer during the riots at Strangeways, he struggles with PTSD.

During the riots, the prisoners on the roof tied t-shirts doused in oil from the kitchen on to 25-foot scaffolding posts, set fire to the T-shirts and then threw the burning posts on to the prison officers below.

He had said that it is impossible to avoid the triggers in everyday life.

He explained that when he walks down the street and sees scaffolding, it triggers memories of the riots and brings back all the difficult, frightening experiences of the prison and his time in the army. But, over time, he has developed coping mechanisms that allow him to handle the triggers.

There are so many different types of anxiety and stress, some invoke mental trauma, others physical difficulties and each have their own unique, individual triggers.

After speaking to the man for a few minutes, Coco decided that she was ok to walk home and, on the way, I pondered the message the man had shared with me and how I could apply it to my anxieties.

I concluded that recognising the triggers is the first step but developing coping mechanisms is the key to dealing with the associated anxiety. Easier said than done but, as the man had proved, not impossible.

If that man hadn't travelled from Rochdale, if I had left earlier, if Grandad Bob hadn't left at the same time and, most importantly, if Coco hadn't refused to walk, the conversation would not have happened, and the words of wisdom wouldn't have been shared. Coco had created the opportunity for the lift that I needed. Dogs do work in mysterious ways.

By the way, the man wasn't dressed all in white with angelic wings, but he did have an Ozzy Osbourne-style cross round his neck ... thankfully it wasn't upside down!

"Selfish forgiveness... it's your future!"

"Take control, sit, wait, seize your opportunities, stand your ground, and don't be intimidated!"

"Anger will not change the hurt from the past but it will prolong it!"

Cathartic Writing

27th July 2017

"I am wolf. Quietly I will endure. Silently I will suffer. Patiently I will wait.
For I am a Warrior. And I will survive."

"From the outside looking in, it's hard to understand.
From the inside looking out, it's hard to explain"

Over the past few weeks, as part of my recovery from my latest attack of anxiety, I've taken some time to revisit the difficult years that I've been through and, by writing my scrambled, well-rehearsed thoughts down on paper, I've brought some structure to the mess that's been in my head for so long.

As well as being very cathartic, the process was also very shocking and difficult but also helped me realise, again, especially compared to other people's stories, how blessed, thankful, and incredibly lucky I am to still be capable of writing this post.

The first quote above, from a Facebook group about Wolff-Parkinson-White syndrome helps to convey the inner strength I have gleaned, from the lifelong battle with WPW, to continue to function, to work, to support, to nurture, and to live, despite everything.

The second quote sums up perfectly the quandary this invisible battle and resultant strength portrays to the outside world.

At the moment, emotions are running high in my mind as I seek closure to this very long-running invisible battle, but I can see the light in the very black sky that is slowly moving away as I continue to walk my line.

I am a wolf!

Stay strong.

"The power to lift yourself, is the greatest strength of all!"

"If something is said, don't let it go to your head.

When your conscious is clear, you have nothing to fear.

People will judge, but there's no need to budge.

Your path is true, and so are you!"

Admission

With the backing of the company doctor, I looked forward to changes being made at work, leading to alterations to the culture, better system support and improved mental health engagement.

A few weeks after I received the letter from the Doctor, a meeting was arranged with HR. Before the meeting I decided to write down everything I'd discussed at my appointment but in greater detail. None of the contents should have been a surprise to those who read it.

We started the meeting by going through the doctor's letter, addressing his concerns about my problems commencing in 2010. It was suggested that all the work on that project was performed by a company from Germany, there was no reason for me to feel stressed.

I mentioned that I had been working on my own, with very little support, for long periods on old, complex, critical, and fragile systems with very little peer assistance and nobody to watch my back.

I was shocked that they didn't remember how badly I was affected and how stressed I had become, especially when I was implementing the changes on my own.

We continued through the letter. I ensured that every attempt to reduce the severity of my stress levels were answered and gave my version of everything.

As the review of the letter ended, I mentioned how I felt when Doctor Andrews diagnosed his concerns about my mental health issues. The other attendees were surprised, and it seemed that they didn't realise that the doctor had said anything about poor mental health. I pointed to the sentence on the last page of the letter –

"I have concern regarding his degree of mental resilience and psychological vulnerability."

As the meeting ended, I produced a document outlining, in detail, everything that I'd been through since 2010. Raising questions about the stressful time I had experienced especially between 2012 and 2015.

It was then that I was handed the leaflet for a free telephone counselling service and told to contact the counselling service and arrange counselling myself. I was also to see my GP and get a referral to a cardiologist as recommended by Doctor Andrews.

At the end of the meeting as I got up to leave, the other attendees decided that they needed to talk without me present, so I left the room and returned to my desk.

It was time to concentrate on the support outlined by Doctor Andrews.

The company doctor had set me on a different path, a path that I hoped would lead to closure from seven years of pain, uncertainty, fear, and unexpected challenges.

What I didn't realise at the time is how long and protracted the journey to closure would be, how there would be many twists and turns and how I'd have to make most of that journey unaided.

For my previous heart operations, I had to rely on the skills and talents of the surgeons, for this recovery I had to do most of the work on my own.

Given the sensitive nature of the subject, I decided not to discuss any of my challenges with anyone else at work, only the people involved in the meeting, plus Senior Management, were aware of my story and planned recovery.

This self-imposed silence would hamper and often threaten to derail my recovery and the frustration was instrumental in prolonging the initial steps along the path.

I followed the recommendations from the company doctor but there was no structure in place at work to ensure that my well-being was ok, and single-handedly I went through the investigations and counselling sessions over the next few months.

During the Counselling period, I passed my 32nd Anniversary in the same employment.

In that time, I'd delivered numerous projects that had resulted in robust, flexible, and easily maintainable systems that provided numerous benefits and cost savings with minimal problems and rework required. My successes made the response to my challenges even harder to fathom.

As I was feeling more settled, I was able to reduce the number of days I worked from home but every day I spent in the office became more challenging.

As I was spending most of my time trying to come to terms with the diagnosis and trying to plan and prepare for the steps I had to take, I didn't feel able or be the one to reach out.

Gradually, as I started to recover, the feelings of anger, resentment, bitterness and frustration that surrounded the time, fitness and confidence that I had lost increased.

These feelings would lead to a major turning point in my story, a decision that would change everything.

"Sometimes you have to test the water, to see who will save you from drowning.

If no one steps forward to help, learn to swim by yourself!"

"It's better to be a victim of your own success than a slave to someone else's. Take control!"

"Self-motivation: selfless perseverance to do your best in everything you do and 'carry on regardless', even though you know that, while everyone else gets away with murder, you get away with nothing!"

August 2017

Master of Your Fate

5th August 2017

Four years ago, the build-up of stress finally broke through my dam of resistance and my latest battle commenced.

Finally, I've been given the opportunity to tell my story.

I don't know what will come out of the next few weeks but by working through this process, I feel closure may be on the horizon…

Reconcile your thoughts ✓

Quell your anger ✓

Dilute your bitterness ✓

Forgive your antagonists ✓

Release your chains ✓

Remove your weight ✓

Master your fate! ✓

Or as the Great Ozzy Osbourne encapsulated so aptly, maybe it's the "End Of The Beginning".

"Rise up, resist and be the Master of your fate!"

First Steps

8th August 2017

Quite a day…worked from home until 12.40 this morning which involved one or two stressful moments and woke up with my heart throwing in a few extra beats as a consequence.

Had another brilliant time at Holiday Club where my heart returned to its normal beat – extra beats hate exercise – thanks kids!

I took a phone call from a counselling service who are going to sort out some counselling for the stuff I've been through over the last few years.

I went to see a cardiologist who told me my heart was working as expected and the stress-related palpitations don't appear to have caused any additional problems.

And to finish off, a lovely meal at The Office Restaurant with my amazingly supportive family!

Roller Coaster

13th August 2017

Post from 13th August 2015:

Today has been one of those roller coaster of emotion days.

The euphoria and pride of finding out Jake's results and hearing of all the other young people, whose paths I've crossed in various different ways, moving on to bigger and better things and the reminders of how far I've come in my recovery from the lows I've been through.

I love the way fate has impeccable timing. Not long after Jake had got his results, Timehop delivered a text message that I'd sent to work two years ago, explaining the difficulties I was having with my heart following a very stressful and tiring project. Five days of constant ectopic (extra) heartbeats, unable to sleep, battling to keep myself going but only making myself worse.

And here I am two years later, still improving each day, near to my target weight (that's taken ages to achieve) and realising now just how poorly I've been for the last five or so years.

Two years on from this roller coaster status and the battle for stability in my heart and answers to my questions goes on.

But the roller coaster has slowed down and flattened out.

Jake and Sam are doing amazing in everything they do, from University, college, and work to being integral parts of last week's amazing Holiday Club.

And I've seized the opportunity provided to instigate counselling to deal with the past seven years that led to my stress and anxiety-induced heart problems.

I've arranged appointments with the cardiologist, and subsequent Echocardiogram, which will hopefully provide reassurances that despite everything my heart has been through over the fifty-two years of its life, no damage has been caused by the latest attacks on it.

I'll be speaking to the company doctor again on Wednesday and I'm sure the time I took to write down my experiences over the last few years will come up in discussion.

As part of my heart checks, I've been given a heart recorder to try and capture a bout of palpitations in action so the cardiologist can work out their type, cause, and treatment.

Over last few days, because I feel a lot more stable, I've been really busy (Holiday Club BBQ and finale, ten-mile walk, battering the back garden etc.) and my heart has performed magnificently.

Tomorrow, after a few days holiday, I return back to work and, let's just say, that if I need to use the recorder while I'm sat at my desk, the noises it makes as the electrodes pick the erratic beats will make for very interested listening!

It's time I closed the ride! 😁

Cardiology

Before I could make the decision to forgive, I had to discover if my heart had been damaged by the years of stress, anxiety and palpitations.

I love having a life-long, very close relationship with my heart. We've been through so much together.

I can tell when it is having a bad day, having a moment, or when it's happy and settled.

Given its history, I've become very aware of its every move and I often get pre-occupied with its idiosyncrasies. When it is very well behaved, quiet, and unnoticeable, I can reduce the monitoring and dim my awareness.

In 2013, when the stress triggered a first bout of palpitations in seven years, it immediately raised my anxiety levels. The irregularity of the beats, the length of time since my last bout of SVT, and the fact that it occurred when I was implementing a challenging project at work, sent the monitoring into overdrive.

Unfortunately, even though the palpitations made concentration almost impossible, I had to continue to work and, knowing that I would have to persevere for another twelve hours, this only served to make the bout more severe.

After a few hours of hoping that my heart would reset itself and not having the confidence to implement the Valsalva Manoeuvre, I realised that the fear and uncertainty that surrounded a part of the implementation had triggered the palpitations.

Almost immediately after I'd decided to rescope and reduce the complexity of the implementation, my heart reset itself and I was able, albeit very cautiously, to complete the implementation but the psychological damage had already been instigated.

Over the next few years, the anxiety, together with unrelentingly high levels of stress, caused a wide variety of palpitations.

Recognising the fear of my own heart that had developed over the previous four years, the first step that the company doctor recommended was a cardiology check-up. He knew that if the cardiologist tests were positive, this would have a dramatic effect on my recovery from mental illness.

Given that long term exposure to high levels of stress can lead to cardiac arrest, strokes/seizures caused by blood clots generated by the irregular heartbeat and heart failure, I viewed the visit to the cardiologist with a great deal of trepidation.

When my cardiologist explained what he was looking for, I became fully aware of the extent of the damage that could have been caused.

Stretching of the heart's chambers, caused by an enlarged, under stress heart, which could lead to heart failure, and a possible heart transplant.

A back-up of fluid, caused by blocked arteries, leading to a bypass operation.

Atrial Fibrillation, which could cause blood clots to build in my blood stream, possibly leading to cardiac arrest or a stroke.

Thankfully, my concerns were unfounded as, after an ECG and Echocardiogram, I received the all clear from the cardiologist on my 25th Wedding Anniversary.

I was very emotional when I discovered that my heart hadn't suffered any damage from the years of avoidable stress and, for the first time in months, I could begin to see a distant glimpse of closure.

Little did I know, at the time, that the distance would take a long time to traverse.

All Clear

29th August 2017

Just been given the great news by my cardiologist that the Echocardiogram I had a few weeks ago has shown that no damage was caused by the last seven years of work-related stress and the major bouts of palpitations that I experienced as a result.

I'm so proud of my (not so) dicky ticker, especially considering how much it has been through in its life.

Now to get closure to everything I've been through. I feel incredibly thankful to still be here to say this but…it's time!

"Positivity > Negativity, do the maths."

"Don't live your life by someone else's book, write your own!"

"A true friend just wants their friends to be happy, loved, and safe... no matter the circumstances and distance that may keep them apart!"

September 2017

Relaxed Exercise

3rd September 2017

One of the hardest things about any heart scare is the recovery of confidence that is quickly lost when you suffer an attack, however severe or however long.

Standing up from the sofa, getting out of bed, climbing the stairs and walking the dog all become a challenge that you need to conquer to increase your confidence, not knowing if the next step could cause a repeat attack.

After my visit to the cardiologist's on Tuesday I'd been suffering with ectopic (extra) beats due to the build of stress and anxiety as I waited to find out about the results of my Echocardiogram. Results that would have a massive impact on my life, either positively or negatively.

Ectopic beats, although usually benign, are difficult to live with, they randomly occur and can be felt as an extra strong beat in addition to your normal beats. You are not sure when they have finished as they can disappear for minutes then catch you by surprise. The tension they create just adds to the problem and this leads to increased anxiety, tiredness, and, despite the positive results of my Echocardiogram, reduced confidence in the functioning of my heart.

Although Kay had done most of the organising for our Silver Wedding Anniversary party, I was on edge as it approached. I wanted the night to go smoothly, for everyone to have a brilliant time, but the thought of the ectopic beats leading to a more severe attack of arrhythmia, while I was setting up, doing my speech or dad dancing, was at the forefront of my mind.

Then I went on a relaxed walk with Coco yesterday.

I've found over time that for me, the most difficult part of any time of exercise is soon after I finish and start to relax. That's when, as the adrenaline starts to reduce, my palpitations have, in the past, kicked in and lasted for hours.

But yesterday was different. As I sat and ate my Shredded Wheat, I noticed that the ectopic beats had stopped. I waited for them to catch me out but as time went on, I became more confident they had finally stopped, and I could look forward with more confidence to the evening ahead.

Obviously, as the night commenced and progressed, I was very conscious of my heart.

As I danced, I would be listening to my heart over the cheesy disco music.

When I started to overheat, I took myself outside to calm down and bring my pulse down, from its normally raised beat. Still no ectopics or arrhythmia.

The rest of the night passed peacefully and, although I was holding back on the mad dancing, as the sweat patches proved, I was still pushing things as far I as felt safe to do.

Then, as we packed up and set off home, I was prepared for the after-effects.

At home I sat down, waiting, not wanting to go to bed because lying down always had an adverse effect on my heartbeat. I eventually got to bed and despite a slightly restless beat as my body calmed down, nothing more severe.

I was up at 7.30 the next morning … and all I could feel was the wonderful feeling of Sinus Rhythm.

Onwards and upwards!

"May light overcome the darkness and love banish the pain."

"Listen to the quiet ones, by their very nature they choose their words more carefully.
Cool, calm, controlled and clinical!"

Moving on

A few days after my initial cardiology check-up, I had an impromptu chat at work which brought into focus that there was little likelihood of a response to my struggles and that the company doctor's recommendations may not be implemented.

My response was appropriately abrupt, terse, and angry. I was livid, the bitterness, anger, frustration, and resentment that I'd been feeling for a few weeks reached boiling point. I could feel my heart rate start to increase, my blood pressure shot up and I felt completely let down.

The following day, I realised that the previous day's conversation had started to have an adverse effect on my health, and I had a difficult choice to make. Continue the fight for a response or concentrate on my health.

As I walked across a field towards a wood with my dog, the decision whizzed around my mind. The positive check-up had given me a boost and brought a bit of light in the dark that had surrounded me for too long.

Then it hit me, I only had one choice, one option, one chance of progress in my recovery.

To decide to follow the path that would continue to improve my health.

As I approached the wood, I chose to move on in an attempt to recover from my mental illness and step forward.

As a Christian, I believe that forgiveness is the backbone of Christianity and is one of the strongest tools that Christians possess.

But the traditional form of forgiveness, when we feel we must ask for our forgiveness to be accepted, has its difficulties.

What if we can't speak to the person that we are forgiving?

What if they are no longer alive?

What if we have lost touch with them?

What happens if our act of forgiveness is rejected?

What if we are seen as weak?

I then had the idea of employing a technique that I'd used before, it was a form of forgiveness that meant I didn't need to ask anyone for forgiveness, but I could still feel the benefits that would give me the best chance to improve and progress on the path that the company doctor had set me on.

I refer to the technique as "Selfish Forgiveness".

We don't often associate the word "Selfish" to a Christian word like "Forgiveness", but this type of forgiveness is very selfish in that it benefits the forgiver without directly encountering the person who is being forgiven.

The beauty of this type of forgiveness is that you don't need to tell the other person that you are forgiving them. Because that requirement is not necessary, there is no fear of rejection, no evidence of being weak in the other person's eyes and no apparent backing down.

But by deciding to forgive someone selfishly, the chains and weight that the other person has placed on you fall off. Your mind becomes focussed and the bitterness, anger, resentment, frustration, and disappointment start to reduce, allowing you to have a clearer mind to work on your progress instead of being held back by the inadequacies of others.

I soon as I made this decision a sense of enriching positivity spread throughout my body and eased the grip of the destructive negativity that had taken hold.

Making the decision to selfishly forgive another person is only half the story, you also need to ensure that it has an effect on your personality and demeanour going forward.

By replacing the negativity with positivity, you feel more able to make changes to the way you approach situations. It is very important to change the way you are when you are in situations with the other person. In doing so the other person will recognise that you are strong, undeterred, and unaffected by their actions or inaction. And then they may realise that you have forgiven them, but that is not a prerequisite to your progress.

I believe this decision was a major turning point in my recovery, by removing the chains that had been burdening me for so long, I was able to start to take back control of my journey. I had wrestled back control; I'd taken the next step to "master my own fate".

I'm so glad that I made that decision on the entrance to the wood.

"The moment you realise that life is too short to allow other people's failings, inadequacies, and deficiencies to affect you; the bitterness, anger, pain, and frustration disappear, your mind is at rest, your heart is at peace and the grimace is replaced with a smirk!"

In a few weeks' time, I would start six hourly sessions with a counsellor, sessions that would drastically change my outlook, my path, and my recovery.

"They might not admit it and you might not think it but sometimes even the strong need a hand to get along!"

"I am a pebble on the riverbed, watching and aware, not caught in the stream!"

"Never give up, everything can change, the spark can return and burn very brightly!"

Counselling

Road to Recovery

9th September 2017

At the start of August, I mentioned that even though I didn't know what the following few weeks would bring, by working through a six-step recovery process, I would, hopefully, move closer to closure from the last seven years of problems.

Over the last few weeks I've made massive progress on my road to recovery and ticked off five of the steps.

The final step, to remove the weight, will happen this week when I see HR for the first time in six weeks on Wednesday followed by my first visit to speak to my counsellor after work.

Should be interesting!

I nervously viewed my first Counselling Session with trepidation and uncertainty.

I'd never needed Counselling to manage my challenges before and couldn't see how sitting talking to someone else could have an impact on what I believed, despite the positive cardiology check-up, was still purely a physical problem.

The stoicism and stubbornness, that I'd relied on to deal with my two heart operations and the myriad of heart palpitations, tried to convince me that counselling would be a retrograde, unnecessary step and an admission that I'd failed, justifying the conception that I was too weak to cope with modern day stresses and strains.

To try to reduce any unexpected surprises, I've always made sure that I'm fully prepared for meetings or presentations.

Before the first counselling session, I spent a great deal of time compiling copious notes about my battles. Continuing from the discussion with the company doctor, I concentrated on the time from 2010 to 2017.

As I relived the challenges, the sheer emotion of my struggles brought greater fear and anxiety about the first counselling session. If it was hard enough to write my thoughts down, how will I be able to cope speaking about it to a stranger.

The nervousness grew as I drove over to the Royal Preston Hospital.

Finding a parking space, locating the correct building, booking into reception, and waiting in an empty Waiting Room only increased my levels of anxiety to a peak. My heart was racing, my fear was in control.

As soon as Dr Laraway appeared in the Waiting Room and shook me by the hand, a feeling of peace and light started to overcome the fear and the darkness. A feeling that would grow over the next six weeks as we systematically analysed everything that had happened up to that point. No stone was left unturned, no subject off bounds, everything was on the table.

We started by talking about my recent flare up of anxiety and then naturally progressed on to the historical reasons for my anxiety caused by the stress-induced palpitations that I have been encountering over a long period of time. During the discussions I handed Dr Laraway the statement that I had written following the first letter from Dr Andrews, the two letters that Dr Andrews had sent me, and a document outlining the steps I have taken to aid my recovery.

Dr Laraway seemed to completely understand what I've been going through and related it to psychosomatic problems combined with a physical history of difficulties that cause a cyclic effect of anxiety that affects my mind, body, and heart.

He provided me with two CDs, one on relaxation techniques and the other on mindfulness through breathing. He suggested that I attempt all the techniques on the CDs and decide which ones, after practice, are most beneficial to my needs.

At the end of the session I felt a great sense of relief.

At the next session, building on the first session, we discussed a whole raft of different situations that I've been through – all relating back to my concerns about my heart and how my anxiety/thoughts/experiences have been affecting it and making me feel like I've lost control, severely denting my confidence.

He confirmed that everything I've been doing so far has been the right thing to do and that I was going in the right direction.

He told me that, following on from the all-clear from the cardiologist, I should look to start to "challenge" the anxiety by putting together a five- to six-step plan to reach a goal that will gradually take me out of my comfort zone. He said that if I just carry on like I have been doing, the anxiety will reduce but, without challenging it, it may hang around waiting to come back.

We then discussed the possible goals and how I can go about reaching them, while using the relaxation/breathing techniques that I'm practising.

The thought of challenging the very thing that had caused me so many problems filled me with dread and, with only some untried techniques to rely on, I felt very vulnerable and exposed.

At the end of the session I asked him if he'd had chance to go through the documents that I'd shared at the first session. He said that he'd been through most of it but then went on to say that to regain control of a situation that I can't really control, that I should concentrate more on improving my health and not let the past hold me back. I said that I'd already started moving on.

I think that was one of the biggest and best decisions I made as it freed me up from the burdens that had been placed on me and I would no longer be held to ransom and I then could start to get my strength, confidence and control back.

At the next session, we started talking about how I have been feeling over the previous week and I informed Dr Laraway that it had been a bit of a roller coaster with highs, lows, and numerous revelations.

On the Thursday of the previous week, I woke to my heart beating very quietly, something that has happened on rare occasions in the past and the difference this normal beat makes to my psyche is very dramatic.

On previous occasions, the wonderful feeling has been tinged with uncertainty as to how long the feeling will continue as there was no certainty that my heartbeat would continue this way. But this time felt more permanent especially given the news from my cardiologist and the advice and guidance I'd received from Dr Laraway.

However, shortly after my lunch and while I was sat at my desk, my heart suddenly started beating faster and stronger.

Usually, I would react with dread and tension to my raised heartbeat but this time I picked one of the breathing techniques that were included on the CDs that Dr Laraway had given me.

The technique advises control of my breathing and instead of becoming hardened and tense to the discomfort of my palpitations to simply acknowledge their presence and treat them with sensitivity and kindness by breathing in sensitivity and breathing out the resistance.

I was a little sceptical that this would work as it all seemed too simple but within a couple of seconds the palpitations stopped, and my heart returned to the quiet beat from the morning.

The technique had dealt with the anxiety before it had chance to take hold and increase the severity and length of the bout of palpitations. This was a major revelation to me and gave me more confidence that I could now deal with any future episodes of palpitations.

My heart continued to beat quietly throughout the rest of Thursday, all day Friday, and the start of Saturday.

After completing my eight-mile walk on Saturday, I sat down to relax and eat my breakfast. Again, my heart started doing extra ectopic beats which were stronger than the normal beats.

I sat quietly and controlled the natural feeling of hardness and tension through the breathing technique and, as happened on the Thursday, my heartbeat returned to the quiet beat within a few minutes. Further evidence that I now had more control of how I reacted to the episodes and a big step forward in making the wonderful feeling I was experiencing more permanent.

However, the quiet heartbeat and the possibility of it becoming permanent was darkened with a major feeling of regret that I had not been feeling like this for a number of years and that reminded me how good I felt in 2009 before the stress increased, leading to complications from 2013 to 2017.

This regret led me to feel increased resentment.

Dr Laraway agreed that this was a perfectly normal reaction to have but I needed to ensure that I controlled the feelings of anger, bitterness, frustration, and resentment so they don't impact the undoubted health benefits that I was starting to experience again.

I agreed that, given how wonderful I was feeling, I didn't want anything else to affect it but that I would need to raise all these issues at the forthcoming meeting with HR. I assured him that I was in a much better position to deal with the situation than I was four weeks previously, i.e. before my cardiologist follow-up appointment and before I started my counselling.

Dr Laraway then asked if I felt there was adequate mental health provision in my company and whether HR and Management know how to handle the situations with poor mental health. I replied that I felt there wasn't a structure in place to deal with psychological issues and by not doing anything they were in danger of making the situations worse. He agreed with this.

I then told him that the last three weeks had been incredibly beneficial but also very tiring and emotional as I had to spend a lot of time reliving moments of my life that I had pushed to the back of my mind.

To allow me to deal with those moments it was important that I addressed them so I could talk to Dr Laraway and finally, hopefully, deal with them. But to have had limited support had made things more difficult.

We finished the session by going through my plan to reach a goal I had set myself. He agreed that my goal and the steps I outlined were achievable and sufficiently gradual but allowed me to stretch myself and challenge the anxiety while applying the techniques I'd learnt when applicable. He advised that as well as challenging my anxiety, as I had been doing when my palpitations started last week, I also need to challenge it physically and keep challenging it at a level I feel comfortable before increasing the physical activity until I reach my goal.

Before I could take my first step, I had to deal with a potentially difficult meeting with HR at work. The meeting would be the first interaction I'd had with HR since my initial meeting at the end of July.

Before the meeting, I decided to send a summary of the progress that I'd made since my diagnosis, i.e. the positive cardiology report, the first few Counselling sessions, and my initial success with mindfulness.

I feared that the meeting, which I hoped would be a step towards closure, threatened to be very confrontational and possibly escalate into a battle that would only prolong and intensify my struggles.

At the Counselling session before the meeting, I discussed my fears and we agreed that the best approach would be to try to reduce the tension and look to constructively address my concerns about the lack of mental health provision in the workplace.

Right up to the night before, I didn't know how I was going to approach the meeting and I went to bed full of uncertainty and anxiety.

In the early hours of the morning, I was woken by a voice telling me to get out of bed, grab my phone and type up what the voice was telling me. This is what I wrote –

I am probably feeling the best that I've felt in a number of years. I feel more in control of my future health and more able to deal with situations that I will face.

The main reason I'm feeling a lot better is because I feel that I've been heard. Dr Andrews, the company doctor, listened, responded and directed, Dr Mennim, my cardiologist, clarified and reassured, and Dr Laraway, my counsellor, analysed and advised. And by being heard I could start to heal.

The healing process has allowed me to look at the root cause of the stress that triggered my palpitations and how that affected me with my individual difficulties and led to the anxiety over my heart's reaction to the situation that had developed.

Using strategies and techniques outlined by my counsellor we were able to find ways to deal with those challenges, break the cycle of anxiety and palpitations and start on the road to recovery. Together we have found ways to help me deal with the regret, bitterness, anger and frustration that naturally occurred and ensure that I'm no longer affected by them and I can protect the wonderful way I feel today and start to look forward. I feel now that closure is nearer.

However, during that process, a number of issues surrounding the handling of mental health in the workplace have come to light that I feel need to be raised and addressed at a departmental and company level to hopefully prevent others struggling in a similar way in the future.

How is mental health viewed in the department and company?

Stress is part of work life, especially in IT, as people every day strive to do what is right and correct with limited resources, limited time and in some cases, limited skills. Some people can take the stress in their stride but others, like myself, who have underlying serious medical conditions, can't cope in the same way.

Has the Company signed up with initiatives set up to tackle mental health issues and discrimination?

Initiatives like "Time for Change" who provide training to employees to become "Champions" in their workplace and help to identify and highlight mental health issues that their colleagues may be facing and therefore change the way their organisation thinks and acts about mental health.

What provision for mental health issues is there available in the workplace?

Have HR and management been given training to identify and correctly handle mental health issues encountered by their staff?

And what lessons can be learned from my experiences and recovery process?

In the morning, I decided to approach the meeting in a non-confrontational way. To arrive early, with just my phone and a bottle of water and no ammunition to respond to possible accusations that may be thrown my way.

I'd take control and calmly read the thoughts written on my phone, to announce that I'd moved nearer to closure and then look to discuss how future support initiatives could be initiated.

The outcome? A different path, a deconfliction, a recovery of control and, unbeknown to me at the time, a sight of possible closure.

This incident gave me a sight of the power of selfish forgiveness that would have a massive impact on my recovery and would allow me to let go of the bitterness, resentment, anger, and disappointment that I felt from the personal loss of so much.

In the last counselling session, I shared a visualisation that I'd created during my first steps towards my goal. The visualisation explained how the stress had caused my heart to react, how that had increased my levels of anxiety which, when it reached excessive levels, also triggered my heart to react further, escalating the anxiety and creating the palpitation-anxiety-palpitation cycle.

The visualisation demonstrated that the anxiety had reduced my confidence to a non-existent level, and, because of that, I couldn't use my confidence to drain the anxiety and break the cycle.

When I was heard by the Occupational Health Doctor, I was able to reduce the levels of anxiety, that reduction was increased after the cardiology check-up and further diminished when I started counselling.

The moment that I successfully used the mindfulness technique for the first time, I broke the cycle and provided sufficient breathing space to allow the anxiety to be lowered enough to bring the confidence tap into view.

As my confidence increased, my anxiety reduced. Occasionally, as predicted by my counsellor, I would experience setbacks which would cause my anxiety to grow. The visualisation would allow me to monitor the escalations and use the techniques to bring the setbacks under control. The image would also provide a view on my progress to reduce the anxiety levels.

Looking back and the decision to grasp the opportunity of counselling was the best decision I have made and I'm so glad that I ignored the ignorant pleadings of my stoicism and attended the first session.

Those six weeks changed so much.

"Every child deserves the chance to shine, regardless of ability, challenges, or background."

"When you've taken massive strides along your path, things will undoubtedly occur to make you waiver and you will doubt your progress. But your path is true, and so are you!"

"Sometimes the only person who can sort your head out, is you!"

Facebook Posts

During my struggles, especially when I was out walking, I would think of quotes and sayings that gave me a slight glimpse into my troubles and allow me, in some way, to express the challenges I was facing.

There are several of the quotes included in this book.

To allow me to express exactly what I was thinking, and not to upset anyone else, I wrote the quotes using a pseudonym when I posted them on Facebook.

Following my diagnosis and during the counselling sessions, I began to express my thoughts more extensively and as my confidence grew, I discarded the alias and started to write more narratively, using poetry and descriptive language.

I found this very cathartic and it allowed me to bring structure to my thoughts, to share my experiences, techniques, and progress with others, hopefully providing guidance, and to store my reflections as reminders for future reference.

These posts provide an insight into how my focus improved as my mental well-being recovered and how I gained a greater understanding and different view of my psychological illness.

21st September 2017

As I go through the process of counselling, I'm having to revisit a lot of the difficult situations I've been through over the last several years. And they are bringing a lot of pain and discomfort back into the forefront of my mind.

However, as I progress, there have been two stand-out moments that have occurred recently.

The results of the Echocardiogram which gave me physical evidence that my heart had not been damaged and the realisation that, in order to regain control of something I couldn't control, I had to actually let go of it so I could concentrate on something I can control, improving my health.

At last night's counselling session, my amazing counsellor told me that, following on from the excellent news of my Echocardiogram, that it was time for me to start challenging my anxiety by moving out of my comfort zone.

He set me the task of coming up with a five- to six-step plan to reach a goal that, if I achieved it, would most likely deal with my anxiety once and for all. The alternative is to simply continue as I am, progressing slowly, with the possibility of my anxiety going into hiding only to return later.

I know exactly what goal I am going to aim for and have already come up with a plan to, hopefully, achieve it. My counsellor had warned me that there will be difficulties on the way but, as I was advised yesterday, I'm currently learning relaxation and breathing techniques that I can use to conquer any anxiety attacks that I will undoubtedly encounter on my path. And by winning each battle, I will win the war.

Today, I had another one of those stand-out moments.

Just after I'd finished my delicious Wensleydale cheese butties for my lunch, my heart started beating a bit faster and louder, maybe due to acid reflux stimulating the Vagus nerve.

Taking on board what the counsellor had told me, I decided to listen to one of my breathing techniques on my PC.

The technique advises becoming aware of the discomfort with sensitivity and kindness instead of hardening to the experience. The hardening tries to block out the unpleasant experience which brings resistance and secondary suffering. This can then lead to physical tension, irritation, and emotional difficulties that further exacerbate the experience and, in my case, worsen the palpitations.

Once the pain and discomfort has been acknowledged, the pain can be challenged by breathing in softness and breathing out the resistance.

And it worked, within a few minutes my palpitations had subsided, and the anxiety had been dealt with before it had chance to take hold.

Then as I drove to Asda at lunch time, Strange Glue by Catatonia started playing from my shuffled Spotify playlist and the following lines struck me …

"When faced with my demons, I clothe them and feed them,
And I smile, yes I smile as they're taking me over,
And if I cannot sleep for the secrets I keep,
It's the price I'm willing to meet,
The end of the night never comes too quickly for me."

And then the penny dropped and I realised that, up until that point, I'd been resisting the discomfort, a normal reaction, and by doing so I'd been clothing and feeding my demons and although I was able to "smile" through them, they had taken me over.

Time for a change of approach, time to end their hold on me.

Challenge accepted!

Something Changed

30th September 2017

When I spoke to the company doctor and he listened, something changed.

When I released the chains, something changed.

When I got my Echocardiogram results and all was clear, something changed.

When I spoke to my counsellor and he set me right, something changed.

When I challenged my anxiety and took control, something changed.

When I clear the final hurdle next week and stand my ground, everything will change.

Step by step I'll remove the weight, the time is near!

"Sometimes it's best to keep the peace, just to keep the peace!"

"Don't be pigeonholed, you're not a pigeon."

"Celebrate your differences, you're an endangered species!"

October 2017

Retraining My Brain

2nd October 2017

As I start to physically challenge my anxiety by gradually increasing the intensity of my exercise, mild bouts of palpitations are inevitable. The trick was to train my brain in how to react and therefore deal with the bouts.

As my heart has been incredibly quiet for days, I would notice every extra slightly harder beat or short run of palpitations. While I was awake, my brain was semi-trained to just bat them away and subdue them.

It was usually a different story when a bout started in my sleep.

When I was sleeping, and therefore at my most relaxed and least vigilant, historically, my heart, if it's being mischievous, took advantage.

Last night, while I was dreaming about Sandy Toksvig in an episode of Bake Off, my heart became overexcited and started doing funny beats in my dream. However, that wasn't because of some deep lying and rather strange affection for Sandy but because my brain had switched on to my heart's actual, non-dreamy mischief.

In the past, when I've been woken by my heart doing flippy floppy gymnastics, my reaction was to break out in a hot sweat, become really tense and actually invite the anxiety to take hold. This resulted in a more severe bout, a longer period of being awake and, consequently, the feeling of dread about the long day ahead of tiring, anxiety-driven palpitations, that may escalate further.

That night was different though. As soon as my brain became aware of the mischief, and even though I was still semi-conscious, its recently acquired training kicked in.

Using the relaxation technique, and even though deeper breaths can exacerbate the palps, it calmly acknowledged their presence, soothed them away and I drifted back to sleep.

Perfect Approach

4th October 2017

I love it when my brain wakes me up in the middle of the night because it's analysed everything that is going on in my life at the moment, come up with the perfect approach and was too excited to wait until dawn to tell me about it.

Yesterday I signed a pact with my brain, heart, and soul to NEVER let anything or anyone affect the wonderful way I'm feeling.

Thanks to my brain's night shift, I now have something I've been searching for over the last few months, a plan to bring closure in a calm, controlled and constructive way.

And, like my brain, heart and soul, I couldn't be more excited!

First Step

6th October 2017

Today, I took step one on my way to my goal of physically challenging my anxiety and changing how I deal with the reduced heart confidence that has been drastically affected over the last few years.

As I walked through the sand dunes in Formby, I realised that for the past few years I've not been able to accept that it is perfectly natural that my heartbeat will increase as I exercise.

Up until today when my heart rate increased, due to the low levels of confidence, I would intervene and bring it down to normal level as quickly as possible, to try and prevent palpitations, instead of waiting for the rate to reduce on its own.

On the majority of occasions, this intervention would bring my heart down to sinus rhythm but there was always the possibility that as my heart needed to continue to beat faster, to supply more oxygen and blood to other parts of body, it would fire an ectopic, harder beat which would trigger my heart to go into a faster more erratic beat that would possibly last for hours.

By trying to intervene to calm my heart before it was ready, I had made my heart go into palpitations and that, in the past, had reduced my confidence even more.

I have discovered today that, thanks to my Echocardiogram results and strategies and techniques passed on by my counsellor, the confidence in my heart has started to grow.

By recognising that my insistence in bringing a faster heartbeat to normal beat as soon as possible was the cause of my problems, I started to relax as I reached the top of the sand dune. This simple change was very noticeable, the effect remarkable and I have had no adverse reaction from my heart.

Emotional Connection

9th October 2017

At the end of September, I mentioned that when I obtained closure everything would change, but I didn't think things would change this quickly or this dramatically.

Considering the speed of the transformation, some might question how bad I was in the first place and that is completely understandable. But by removing the weight that had been placed on me and because of the number of revelations that have occurred since 2.05 p.m. on the 4th of October, the anxiety and imagination-driven extreme fear of palpitations has changed into reality enhanced progress.

On Friday when I completed step one, I realised that it was ok for my heart to go fast while I was exercising, and I didn't need to intervene to bring it back to a normal pace. The next step was to turn that realisation into reality.

Ingleton, and its falls, have always played a big part in my life. When my mum and dad had a caravan just outside the village, we used to spend some lovely weekends there, walking the falls in all weathers.

Two times stand out and show the emotional contrast of my connection with the falls.

In 2004, while I was battling my severe bouts of SVT, I took myself to the caravan with Niki Dog to try and force my heart back to normal but when I attempted to do the falls walk, I didn't even make it to the entrance gate before my heart went crazy.

In contrast in 2007, two and a half years after my ablation to fix my WPW and stop the SVT attacks in their tracks, me and Kizzy Dog walked the falls three times in six hours.

For step two on my recovery and applying what I'd realised on the sand dune, I did the falls walk again.

Over the past few years, anyone who has been walking with me may have noticed I'd stop part way up an incline and start tapping my belly. This was an attempt to disguise my raised heartbeat and, in a strange way, to try and intervene and induce a slower beat. This would increase the tension in my body which would continue to affect me long after the walk had finished.

By realising that I didn't need to do that and instead I could relax and let my heart do its job, the walk round the falls was incredible, the feeling of release amazing and the benefits enormous.

It was that good, I did the walk twice, clockwise and anti-clockwise!

Draining the Pot

14th October 2017

Post from 14th October 2013 - *It's soooooo nice to NOT feel my heartbeat... quietest it's been in months! :-)*

Two months after my first attack of palpitations for seven years and the optimism, in this post from 2013, that I may have dealt with the problem, is palpable.

Little did I know that the anxiety pot that had been filling up inside me, for the previous two years, had reached overflow in August 2013, the palpitations were the result and they also kept topping up the pot.

When my heart went quiet, today four years ago, it was so noticeable. I'd have been elated because I'd probably have drained the pot a little to reduce the pressure and possibility of overflow.

Unfortunately, and due to factors beyond my control, this was the first of many false dawns and as the next four years would show, things would get much, much worse.

Today, my heart is very quiet again and in general has been quiet for weeks. Because of this I feel so much more confident that this isn't another false dawn but a more permanent feeling. I feel more in control of my future health.

So, what's changed?

To put it simply, I've started to drain the pot. I've installed, with the help of others, taps at different levels on the pot.

The first tap was installed after being heard and directed by the company doctor. This allowed me to bring the level of anxiety down to a point that meant I had room to start to heal.

The next tap, slightly lower down the pot, was installed after I was reassured by my cardiologist that my heart had not been affected by the stress.

The next few taps, again each positioned slightly lower down the pot, were installed after being analysed and advised by my counsellor. These taps are a result of the techniques, the ability to change approach, and the recognition of reality that he has instilled in me.

I feel the level of my anxiety is now at somewhere around 60% and due to the steps I've taken and changes I made, I'm determined to not let it fill up again. And the newly installed taps will help me prevent that, if necessary.

But with every step I take on my road to recovery, every quiet heart day and every time I manage to deal with a setback or slight dribble of palpitations, I'm relearning how to operate the biggest, most powerful, and permanently installed in all of us tap. The confidence tap.

This tap is situated right at the bottom of our anxiety pots and is used to drain the pot after a period of stress that life throws at all of us which has raised the level of anxiety and usually it allows us to recover. But when the flow of stress is excessive and the anxiety feeds itself by aggravating the physical symptoms, we lose sight of the Confidence Tap, we forget how to operate it and its powerful flow is blocked and stopped.

It takes a long time and a great deal of effort to be able to start to open the Confidence Tap again but the impact on the anxiety is massive. And I'm just starting to feel that.

And by being heard, I could start to heal. Simple really, isn't it?

Reaching Out

21st October 2017

Post from 21st of October 2016 – *I'm glad I took the decision to down tools at work to reduce the stress that caused me so many problems, and as today proved (again!) all my efforts, concerns and worries continue to go unnoticed! But I have control!*

When I posted this status this time last year, I must have been feeling better in myself probably because of my exercise routine and dietary changes, which had made me feel stronger and more in control.

Little did I know at the time, and I've only just found this it out very recently, that no amount of exercise or changes in diet would have dealt with the vast build-up of anxiety that lay in wait for the next trigger.

What I've learned since is the massive effect that anxiety, and the psychological problems that are part and parcel of it, has on my cardiology.

Yesterday, a young mum from North Carolina posted on the amazing Facebook group for sufferers of Wolff-Parkinson-White syndrome that, after multiple tests, she'd recently been diagnosed with WPW. She was concerned about the extra beats that she was getting and wanted to know if that was the WPW or, as her Doctor said, nothing to worry about. Turns out she'd only recently given birth and, as a result, the anxiety she'd been managing since she was 14 had flared up.

Although we are at different stages of our lives, she is the same age as my eldest son, our stories are very similar. It was very uplifting to share my recent experiences and provide reassurances from a fellow sufferer's point of view. I also passed on the relaxation technique that helps me control the extra beats when they occur. Hopefully that will allow her to keep control of her anxiety levels and continue to enjoy being a new mum.

Facebook has its problems but given how much I've recovered since I was heard, reassured, and advised, maybe Facebook has allowed this young person from thousands of miles away to feel the same.

Visualisation
29th October 2017

If you had said to me less than four weeks ago that I could have done all that I've done this weekend, then I'd have told you to give your head a shake.

They say that you only truly know how bad you've been when you feel better and I know now exactly how bad I was just less than four weeks ago and for a long time before that.

So, what's changed?

Well, even though I haven't been able to change what I can't change, I was able to change through "selfish" forgiveness, my approach to those things that had been affecting me and by doing so things changed … dramatically.

I mentioned three weeks ago that I'd managed to visualise what I'd been through and that had helped me understand how it had affected me and to monitor my progress.

I feel now that my anxiety levels are at 50% and because I've reduced that level, I can now see and utilise my confidence tap that had been swamped but will now help me drain the anxiety pot even more.

By reducing the anxiety, my fear of palpitations has reduced massively. Caffeine, alcohol, exercise, and stress do not affect me in such debilitating way as they have done recently and historically.

For the moment, I'm consolidating my current level of exercise and twice this weekend I've walked through the Pinewoods in Ainsdale to build up my fitness levels. I can't wait to take my next step, when we head to Linnett Hill B&B in Keswick in three weeks' time.

Onwards and upwards!

"It's ok to be responsibly irresponsible!"

"Let's start a revolution in our heads..."

"Don't look back in anger...disgust, anxiety, distraction, sorrow, and guilt, look forward with pride, joy, intrigue, trust, love, and peace!"

November 2017

Reality-Based Evidence

2nd November 2017

Post from 2nd Nov 2016:

One of the most liberating moments of your life is when you realise that you don't need to compete with or compare yourself to anyone else. And that all the time wasted on petty, inconsequential, fruitless, and negative quarrels and fallouts is better spent on you growing you and helping those around you to grow too. From that moment on, whatever is thrown at you doesn't stick, hurtful things said to you don't register, what other people think of you doesn't matter and bad things done to you cause no damage. Make the moment, you have no time to waste.

Even though this time last year I thought I had a handle on things, the last few months have proved that I didn't have any idea what was causing me to feel that way.

A year ago, what I was fighting and what was eating me from the inside was invisible to me, but it was, and had been for years prior to that, visible to some others.

A year on and, thanks to the incredible help of a multitude of people, I've not only managed to expose the cause, recognise its most lethal weapon, challenge its right to exist and through reality-based evidence reduce its grip on me.

Over the years, I've doubted my faith, questioned my beliefs and felt very alone but now another quote that I wrote in March 2015 still rings true.

"Being misunderstood by someone who doesn't have a clue, validates your beliefs and verifies your being!"

Third Step

20th November 2017

During my recent counselling sessions, I'd set aside this weekend to take my third step on my road of recovery.

Before we dropped Coco off at the kennels, I mentioned to Mandy, one of the owners of Linnett Hill, that I was anxious about leaving Coco. Anxiety that in the past would probably have tipped me over the edge, especially as I'd been fighting a chesty cough for two weeks, and that would have ruined my weekend.

But now I've managed to reduce the levels of anxiety to a manageable level, I could take Friday's anxiety and the concern about the bug in my stride and complete the fifteen-mile walk on Saturday with ease.

But it's the reaction after the walk that says so much. Rushing back to the kennels to drop Coco off, eating a lovely big meal for Kay's birthday, enjoying a pint of Peroni, and drifting off to sleep with no palpitations and no ectopic beats.

I can't believe how far I've come in six weeks, and it is all down to sorting my head out.

"Replace complexity with simplicity, lies with honesty, isolation with inclusion, intolerance with understanding and suddenly everything becomes easier for everyone."

"Until you talk, listen, and understand, you'll never see!"

"Moments will pass, you will always be you!"

December 2017

Regaining Focus

5th December 2017

As well as taking the anxiety away from my heart, which has changed my whole psyche and allowed me to enjoy an alcoholic drink or a normal tea, getting rid of the mush in my head has resulted in other less obvious but equally uplifting advantages.

Instead of being totally preoccupied by my next heartbeat, forcing my exercise, losing concentration, and being forgetful, I'm starting to regain focus on the important things in life.

Being able to solve problems at work (proving my abilities), remembering events, planning for things in good time, and most importantly, helping my family and friends with their lives and any difficulties they may face.

Things are still raw, and I still get emotional when I realise how far I've come (and just how bad I was), occasionally my heart may be a bit mischievous, but I'm made up with my progress in the last eight weeks.

There have been a lot of important moments that have led to this point. However, sitting at my desk at the end of September, just after eating my lunch, as my heart started beating crazily and realising the power of this simple breathing exercise, was a life-changing moment.

Six Words

27th December 2017

Everyone faces challenges in their lives but sometimes, when everything seems lost, someone will say something that, on the face of it, seems frightening or even inconsequential but changes your whole world.

This year, as in 2004, I've been down a difficult road but, in both cases, six words have changed my destination from a dark, forbidding, scary place to one of light, joy, and beauty.

And, in hindsight, I've realised that I had to travel down the difficult roads to force the issue and be able to change my long-standing situations.

In 2004, after months of uncontrollable palpitations, I was sat on the edge of a hospital bed trying to muster up the courage and strength to walk fifty yards down the corridor when the nurse came past with the medicine trolley.

"You've got Wolff-Parkinson-White Syndrome," she said in an off-the-cuff manner.

In an instant panic set in and the walk was put on hold while I frantically Googled "Wolff-Parkinson-White syndrome". As I investigated more, and following conversations with the cardiologist, it became apparent that the prognosis was far from bleak and that a permanent cure to the syndrome was possible.

The rest is history.

I firmly believe that I was taken down that difficult road to hear those words and to rectify a life-long problem.

This year a similar difficult road led me to the company doctor and from there to a different cardiologist and, for the first time in my life, a counsellor.

During my second counselling session, after my counsellor had read my copious notes and taking into account the positive results of my cardiology check-up, he said these six words – "You need to challenge your anxiety".

I had a similar reaction to when I was sat on the side of my bed as those six words also filled me with dread.

Why would I want to expose my body to the anxiety that had undoubtedly caused me so much suffering over such a long period?

Why should I lay bare my vulnerability and put myself in danger again?

I'd come so far, or so I thought.

Then my counsellor said something that will stay with me for a long time – "You need to see the reality".

And that was the catalyst that I needed to start my fight back.

But that's where the similarities with 2004 end. In 2004 I relied on the skill and judgement of the amazing doctors and surgeons, this year I had to do it all by myself. Nobody else could sort my head out.

And here I am today, just past the best Christmas I've had in years. Yes, I've had a few dodgy moments when my heart reacted slightly to a bit too much Guinness or a bit too much exertion but because I've challenged my anxiety and because I've seen the reality, there is no longer any fuel added to the fire and I can just waft those dodgy moments away.

It's hard to put into words exactly how it feels to not be able to feel my heart. To lie in bed concentrating on feeling it and failing.

It's hard to explain how nice it feels to be able to relax and enjoy the festivities as a "normal" person. To spend time with my family, to choose to have a drink with a good friend or to sample the delights of Danish Blue cheese after a big meal and not pay the price for hours after.

We all travel down difficult roads and I'm sure many of you know people who are on such a road now. Where hope seems lost and everything seems bleak, but I know that six words can change everything. They may not solve all the problems, but they can make the person who is struggling feel a bit more secure during their vulnerable time.

"It's ok, I'm here for you!"

"Positive steps forward build resilience against negative setbacks."

"Help bring some green to someone else's life!"

"Nature ... the free daily restorer and nourisher!"

January 2018

Change in Demeanour

6th January 2018

Three months ago today, I took my first step on my recovery and, especially given the length of time, my progress, thanks to my supportive family and friends, has been profound, surprising, and sometimes emotional.

As well as the invisible changes to my physical and psychological fitness my whole demeanour has changed and, for those willing to see it, it's very noticeable.

However, there are those who, for whatever reason, refuse to engage in or celebrate my recovery. Their silence and inaction speak volumes and provides massive motivation for me to continue to improve and show that I can still do the things that I've been able to do for the last three decades.

I'm now between steps three and four, consolidating my progress and currently having a declutter of my body fat ready for, hopefully, more steps in Spring and Summer.

Another lovely walk in the trees and dunes this morning.

Coco also showed progress in her battle against her anxiety by shrugging off two major triggers, gun shots in Formby Hall and the plane noise from Woodvale.

Power of Forgiveness

12th January 2018

It felt good to finally give an update on my progress today and air my views on the causes behind my problems over the last eight years.

For the last few months, I've enjoyed feeling positive about my future and witnessing the power of forgiveness in action. However, that forgiveness does tend to leave a bit of a bad taste in my mouth.

But I'm not going to let the slight bad taste affect how well I'm feeling.

Then this quote popped up from something I posted on this day last year:

"The knowledge that you have emerged wiser and stronger from setbacks means that you are, ever after, secure in your ability to survive. You will never truly know yourself, or the strength of your relationships, until both have been tested by adversity. Such knowledge is a true gift, for all that it is painfully won, and it has been worth more than any qualification I ever earned." ~ J.K. Rowling

All is good!

An Unexpected Visit

14th January 2018

For some reason my good friend the "Delta Wave" reappeared this weekend.

He/she has been in hiding for a few months and, for whatever reason, decided to pay me an unexpected visit.

It's always disconcerting when DW starts triggering extra heartbeats and tries, thankfully unsuccessfully, to reawaken the Wolff and his friends Parkinson and White.

But, and it's a big BUT, things are different since the last visit and despite having a really busy weekend, I've been able to apply my techniques, welcome my previously unwelcome visitor, stay relaxed in its presence, and soothe it and its mischief away.

One of the side-effects of Mr/Mrs D Wave is that it can make me feel very isolated and lonely. As well as the obvious reminders of previous attacks of palpitations, it brings back memories of the anxiety and I search for avenues of solace that might not be open and that can lead to resentment.

And then this morning at Church, we sang a song called "Let Love Be Real" that basically kicked my arse, told me to lift myself and showed that that is the greatest strength of all.

Let Love Be Real - Danny Boy

"Let love be real, in giving and receiving, without the need to manage and to own; a haven free from posing and pretending, where every weakness may be safely known.

Give me your hand, along the desert highway, give me your love wherever we may go.

Let love be real, not grasping or confining, that strange embrace that holds yet sets us free; that helps us face the risk of truly living, and makes us brave to be what we might be.

Give me your strength when all my words are weakness; give me your love in spite of all you know.

Let love be real, with no manipulation, no secret wish to harness or control; let us accept each other's incompleteness, and share the joy of learning to be whole.

Give me your hope through dreams and disappointments; give me your trust when all my failings show."

I'm not sure how long my friend will stay but while it is here, I'll carrying on learning the lessons that it always seems to teach me!

"The power to lift yourself, is the greatest strength of all!"

"Mindfulness: the power to transform anxiety driven 'what ifs, buts and maybes' into reality enforced 'somethings and nothings', restoring focus from unfounded 'fears for the future' to grounded 'here and nows'! And it's as natural as breathing!"

"If beating your Personal Best is sometimes impossible, being your Personal Best is always achievable!"

February 2018

What if?

21st February 2018

Considering I only recently discovered how much damage my battle with mental health had caused, it's perfectly understandable that occasionally the bitterness, anger, frustration, and resentment surrounding my situation will try to resurface.

Today was one of those occasions. Then I stopped and listened to my quiet, almost inaudible heartbeat and a contended smile returned to my face!

A "what if" day, an "onwards and upwards" day, a "if only" day, a "I'm stronger" day, a "Positivity > Negativity" day!

Heart strength

22nd February 2018

This quote has just been posted on a Wolff-Parkinson-White Facebook page.

I'd add "care for your mental health" to the list of things you can do to make your heart's life easier!

This is about your heart.

I have noticed that there are some common misconceptions about the way heart functions, not just here, but in society as a whole.

This is what my cardiologist told me the day after my ablation when I was preparing to leave hospital.

I asked her how long it would take for my heart to regain its strength, as I felt weak. This is what she told me.

Your heart is never weak or strong.

From the moment you are born your heart just does what it does, it supplies oxygen to your muscles. How fast it beats, depends entirely on the demand for oxygen from your muscles. When you are fit your muscles become more efficient at absorbing oxygen from the blood supply and your heart doesn't need to work as hard as it would if you are unfit.

When you are unfit, your muscles are less efficient at absorbing oxygen and consequently your heart has to work harder to supply the required amount of oxygen.

Your heart is never fit or unfit.

It just does what it does from the day you and born to the day you die.

So when you increase your fitness, you are simply making your body more efficient at absorbing oxygen and your heart doesn't need to work as hard.

It's your body that is either strong and efficient, or weak and inefficient. Not your heart, it just does what it has to.

If you have blocked arteries or accessory nerve pathways, once again, your heart still tries to do what it's supposed to do. Your heart will try and go as fast as required, but if that speed extends above its normal capabilities to work properly, i.e. supply blood, then you run the risk of catastrophic heart failure.

Put simply, the only thing you can do to make life easier for your heart is to increase your physical fitness and eat healthy and lead a healthy life.

You can't make your heart fitter, stronger, or indeed change it in any way. All you can do is decrease its workload by making your body more oxygen efficient as a result of exercise and diet.

So the reason I felt weak was that I had been lying in a hospital bed for three weeks. My heart was good to go, as it always is.

Do your heart a favour, get fit and don't make it work as hard.

Flipping and Flopping
27th February 2018

Post from 27th February 2016:

As happens at so many times in my life, for the last few days my mind has been preoccupied by one thing – my heartbeat.

Yes, I have been able to work from home and continue to make decisions and work things through but due to my scar tissue generating an extra beat every 20 seconds, no 30 seconds, no 2 seconds, no 15 seconds, I've really just been surviving.

Sitting on the sofa, trying all sorts of methods to try to fix the problem and just ending becoming more and more tense. Listening, waiting, hoping, and getting more and more anxious and fearful every time I felt the next, thankfully benign, thud in my chest generated by the scar tissue on my heart. I've been quiet, moody, sad, and desperate.

Finding a comfortable position to sleep so as not to aggravate the problem, not sleeping on my left side as I know that's the trigger for more extra beats. As the days and nights went on, you get to think this is permanent until suddenly this morning, when I was out with the dog, the randomly timed extra beats were less noticeable. There wasn't a reaction after I finished my walk as the adrenaline dissipated and slowly, I realised my heartbeat was back to normal.

Within a few minutes my whole demeanour changed, I was chattier, less preoccupied, and less moody. Yeah, I still get a few "aftershocks", but my brain is quieter now and able to think of other things like rebuilding my confidence before my trip to my little bit of paradise in a couple of weeks.

As the children danced and sang at Messy Church this afternoon, I took a moment to listen to my heart beating away in quiet perfection and then enjoyed a hot dog and some apple crumble with my little friends!

I ♡ my ♡ and all the lessons it teaches me!

They say that you don't remember the physical sensation of pain but as I read this post from two years ago I could vividly remember the sensation of my heart flipping and flopping like it did back then. But, thankfully, this time was just a sensation in my head and my heart continues its steady progress back to stability.

Hopefully, snow permitting, I'll be back in Staveley tomorrow night ready to push the boundaries just a little bit more, ready to face any demons and ready to further eradicate the psychological damage from the last seven years.

Like I was in 2005, four months after my ablation, I'm a little nervous to be taking the next step on my recovery but very, very excited, and very blessed to be feeling as good as I do.

"Anxiety is more than just a state of mind."

"Education → Recognition → Understanding → Acceptance → Love → Growth → Education."

"Habit-forming is usually out of your control, can happen in an instant, and has the potential to destroy your life.

Habit-changing is in your own hands, takes time and can transform your life... step by step by step."

March 2018

Plans Scuppered

3rd March 2018

When I was planning my annual visit to Staveley this year, I was going to spend the first couple of days acclimatising to the surroundings, e.g. the inclines, before looking to push my recovery one step further. But I didn't envisage that the acclimatisation would be for very different reasons; the icy, snowy weather.

My plans were not only scuppered, but circumstances forced them to be rewritten.

After two days of walking the same walk – down to the village and back up to the cottage – I've realised that that was the next step I needed to take. And the step was more subtle than trying to climb a mountain, it was recognising the importance of staying relaxed while I walked, not becoming tense and not becoming too excited, as they would all increase my adrenaline and could possibly cause problems after the walk.

And then there was the very enlightening chat with three great friends and the boost that such great friendships can bring.

No more forcing, cramming and rushing. It's time to slide, literally!

Do You Know My Story?

6th March 2018

It was lovely to tag along to Brockhole and Bowness with Jake, Sam, and Kate this morning and catch up with their worlds.

After they'd dropped me off in Staveley, as they headed home, I legged it up the hill to the cottage in record time. Then, instead of watching Tipping Point, me and Coco walked over Green Quarter to Kentmere and got back to the cottage just before dark.

The good thing about coming to the same place year on year is that you can compare things to previous years.

Two years ago, I wrote a poem while I was walking near Staveley. I was obviously thinking my story was coming to an end in 2016, little did I know that there were still plenty of chapters left to write.

Here's the poem I wrote in 2016 and it fits perfectly with what has happened since....

"Do you know my story, my journey to today,

The pain and the suffering that would not go away?

Do you know my story, my journey to this place,

The trials and tribulation edged upon my face?

Do you know my story, my journey to happiness,

Did you celebrate with me, my joy and success?

If you know my story, and helped me on my path,

Thank you for being there, for encouraging me to laugh

If you know my story but hindered or did me wrong,

Please accept my forgiveness, you're one reason why I'm so strong!"

Fitness Test

6th March 2018

Today is my last full day in Staveley and marks the fifth month of my recovery.

Staveley was the fourth step of my action plan agreed with my counsellor in October and, as usual, it has delivered.

182,000 steps, eighty-four miles, thirteen walks up the hill (carrying clothes, chickens, potatoes, milk, flour, teddies etc), a mad dash back before dark and, to finish, a lovely walk through Beckmickle Ing Wood this morning and a walk up Louthrigg Fell this afternoon with sufficient inclines to test my fitness … and it passed!

Poor Understanding

20th March 2018

I can't condone what Ant did when he chose to drive under the influence and hope those involved in the accident would make a full recovery, but the comments made by ITV and Piers Morgan can't be helping Ant in his situation.

Given my experiences, it's obvious that Ant is suffering with severe mental health issues and for ITV to say in their statement that they "hope" he gets the support he needs doesn't go far enough.

Given the amount of money that Ant's skills have earned for the company, they should be doing all they can to ensure that he makes a full recovery before he returns to work and not rushing him back as happened previously.

And then, for the unsubtle Piers Morgan to comment in such an insensitive way about someone he calls his friend is only going to make Ant feel even worse.

In his usually abrasive, uncaring way Morgan blamed Ant for

everything that has happened, that he's "throwing away" his career, causing unnecessary "collateral damage" to Dec and that he is making "bad choices", is another example of poor understanding and awareness of mental illness in society.

My heart goes out to Ant and I hope and pray that he gets the time and support to make a full recovery, that he returns to his career when he is ready, and he's properly supported on his return.

Time to Muster

26th March 2018

A week last Sunday I led the evening service at my Church and shared my story of my mental health problems that had been caused by excessive levels of unmanaged work-related stress.

By sharing my story, I wanted to bring closure to what I'd been subjected to and to try and start to move on with my future.

On the whole that's what I achieved but since sharing my story, my thoughts have turned to the cost of the avoidable situation that occurred through no fault of my own.

It's difficult to quantify the cost as it isn't a tangible amount that can be expressed in monetary terms. However, to obtain total closure I need to face and completely address the bitterness, resentment, anger, and disappointment that I've managed to keep at bay using forgiveness, but I know continues to fester in my psyche. In a similar way to when I challenged my anxiety, if I don't address these issues, they will never leave me and could flare up at any moment.

In 2009, my fitness was probably the best it had been in my life. No SVT palpitations, no restrictions on my exercise levels, endless energy, growing strength and confidence, and no fear of the physical side of sport. My future health was incredibly rosy.

If my fitness trajectory had continued on the same path that it had since my ablation in 2004 by now I'd be super fit and, given my determination to make up for lost time, I would probably be completing all manner of challenges that unfortunately now are pure fantasy.

But the cost is not just limited to my physical fitness but also the increased confidence that physical fitness can bring. Increased confidence to take on more challenging roles at work, for example, pushing for promotions, greater visibility, greater respect, greater standing, greater responsibility, greater recognition, and greater remuneration with all the advantages to my family life that would undoubtedly bring.

And that brings me onto the biggest cost to me personally from the last seven difficult and challenging years, the cost of time and, in particular, precious family time.

If I was 18 when this situation started, I'd be 25 now and still have a lot of years ahead of me to recover my health, fitness, confidence, and career but the same can't be said for someone who will be 53 in October. Yes, I've taken great strides in improving my health and fitness since last October, but my body is not 25 anymore and that brings in to focus the limitations of a body that has already been through so much.

How far can I safely push it?

How will it respond?

What damage could I cause?

Time for my family and closest friends has always been important to me and I've done all I can to protect that time while I've been struggling but there is no doubt that they have suffered.

The total preoccupation with my struggles, my times of incapacitation, my mood swings, my physical limitations have all had an impact on my family and friends. I know that my ramblings on Facebook, as I grappled to understand my mental health, has cost me friendships due to misunderstanding and misinterpretations. Friendships that are now very difficult to repair.

How would my family and friends have benefited if the situation hadn't occurred and I'd continued to grow and flourish?

Although damaged, my health has improved recently and so, therefore, has my strength but I've also developed traits that, although proved useful in my fight, are not the type of traits that I take pride in. I've become embittered, hardened, forthright, overly assertive, scarred and, in some ways, nasty.

These traits are all a result of the fight that I hoped to end during that Sunday evening at Church. People say that fight is all in the past and I need to move on but, as with a lot of mental health issues, that is easier said than done.

Currently my mind is awash with unanswerable questions, "What if?", "If only?", "Why?" "How?", as I fight another battle with my head and the damage that has been caused.

When my counsellor told me to challenge my anxiety, that filled me with dread, but I came up with a plan that showed incredible results in a very short time.

Although I haven't reached the goal of that plan, I feel that it is time to create a new plan to deal with the bitterness, anger, resentment and disappointment that has changed my persona.

My new plan needs to use the things that I've tried my best to keep hold of, my positivity, my ability to see beauty in the simple things in life, my success in reducing the anxiety to a level that means it has little effect in my life now and the undoubted power of forgiveness with strength.

But this fight is different to the fight against my anxiety.

In that battle, I could feel the benefits almost instantly in how my heart started to behave and those benefits quickly snow balled into more positives and bigger benefits. This fight is less physical and more mental and therefore the progress is more difficult to recognise.

So, the battle lines have been drawn, it's time to take on a different, more concealed, more devious and more determined enemy but as the sun streams through the window on this second day of Spring, I feel positive and ready for the fight.

It's time to muster, it's time to move.

Enemy Exposed

27th March 2018

Thanks everyone for your likes, comments, and concern on yesterday's post.

There were two reasons I posted yesterday, firstly so I could bring some structure to my thoughts and secondly so I could publicly expose the issues that I need to address.

By exposing, or flushing out, the enemy, I can now deal with it in a similar way I dealt with the anxiety after my counsellor told me to expose, challenge and destroy that issue.

I know, given my progress against my anxiety, that I couldn't just simply turn away from the other issues that fester in the shadows. Believe me when I say that there are too many triggers in everyday life that bring those issues to the fore and make me react in a negative way. Now I can proactively address these issues in a calm, positive, accepting, and sensitive way and then destroy them with the reality that surrounds me.

It's a similar approach to when you realise that you need to lose weight. You can't lose weight by ignoring the problem, you first need to acknowledge that there is weight to be lost, then come up with a plan to reduce it. The same applies to psychological weight that needs shedding.

Soon after I posted my thoughts yesterday, I recognised a change in my persona, and I felt that I'd taken a big step in the right direction. The enemy is exposed, the issues flushed out and now it's time to systematically take them apart.

"Mindfulness is recognising that instead of forcing and fighting things that you don't understand, you start to understand that you don't need to fight and force things anymore."

"Setbacks show how bad you were, how far you've come and where you've yet to go!"

April 2018

Different Feel

7th April 2018

A week or so ago, I mentioned a battle that I'd initiated against the issues that lingered from my recent mental health problems.

Last week the battle reached tipping point as I progressed to deal with the "What if?", "If Only" and "Maybe" questions that were filling my mind.

A song played on my shuffled Spotify playlist on Thursday by a duo from Brighton called Bitter Ruin. I'd never heard their song "Child in a sea cave" before but the starkness and aggression of its lyrics and the power, intensity, and range of Georgia Train's vocals really hit home and inspired me to write a poem about my current battle.

The first part of the poem looks at all the negative things that I have been facing, allowing me to address them and bring structure to my thoughts and then the second part destroys the issues with definite, positive, realities that I've discovered during my journey.

I've thought long and hard about posting this poem because I don't want to upset people or appear that my story is something different to battles that other people are facing.

Hopefully you'll understand why I need to post it and if it helps one other person who is fighting an invisible battle then it will be worth it.

It's called – "Maybe it would've been different."

"Maybe it would've been different if my scars were there for all to see

What if the wounds weren't all inside of me?

Maybe it would've been different if there had been visible signs of pain

What if they'd helped me become me again?

Just think how it would've been if my heart chambers were distended

What if my life-giving fluid had arrested?

Just think how it would've been if my arteries had furred

What if Atrial Fibrillation had occurred?

I know it became different when God chose to intervene

I know it became different when the doctor had seen

I know it became different when the counsellor did advise

I know it became different cos I'd seen death before my eyes

I know it was different because I was too strong

I know it was different because I'd fought for so long

I know it was different because I have great friends

I know it was different because they helped make amends

I know it was different because I stayed positive

I know it was different because I loved to live

I know it was different because I got help from above

I know it was different because I'd been shown love

I know I feel different because I'm more capable, more forgiving

I know I feel different because I'm more aware, more understanding

I know I feel different because I'm more stable, more loving

I know I feel different because I'm more calm, more giving

I know I feel different because I'm more positive, more me

And that difference is there for all that choose to see

Light has overcome the darkness again

And love has banished the pain."

Lack of Awareness

9th April 2018

Really enjoyed the walk from Downham over Pendle and back - six miles in two hours and a great cardio workout.

The big difference I noticed is the lack of awareness of my heart when I was walking and the lack of reaction and tension after I'd finished, it feels like a brand new me!

And I saw the first ducklings of Spring!

Greater Determination

10th April 2018

I started to think this when I went up that sand dune on October the 6th but last night has proved it even more. There is nothing wrong with my heart and, since my ablation in 2004, there never has been!

There is no way that my heart could recover and repair itself from the distended heart chambers or Atrial Fibrillation or blocked arteries that the cardiologist was checking for in August last year.

The "damage" was all caused by the psychological effects of excessive, unrelenting, and all-encompassing stress which convinced my mind that my heart was physically broken!

I may have lost 20lbs of physical weight but the amount of psychological weight I've shed over the last six months is immeasurable!

Next week I'm giving two talks on my battle with mental health to my colleagues at work.

I've worded the presentation so it isn't a revenge-filled, finger-pointing, blame-riddled rant but hopefully it will be an enlightening, constructive, and culture-changing demonstration of the power of the mind over the body.

After this morning's epiphany, I'm even more determined to go through with the presentations and make changes.

"I will cry repeatedly

But I'll come out the other side a brand new me." ~ Bitter Ruin

Memories Challenged

11th April 2018

Post from 11th April 2015:

I've thought long and hard about posting this, I don't like to dwell on or publicise the negative side of my health issues.

I know there are people who are worse off than me and I don't want family and friends worrying unduly. But I think it's time I came clean and shared some of my experiences, and one in particular that happened exactly one year ago today.

The current slogan for the British Heart Foundation is "Fight for every heartbeat" and it's a slogan that sums up the majority of my life.

Looking back over the past 50 years, I think there are only a few years when I could say that I haven't been fighting, in some way, for every heartbeat.

For those of you who don't know, I was born with a hole-in-the-heart which required open heart surgery. For the first seven years of my life (which I don't remember very well) I survived while I became bigger and stronger to allow the heart operation to take place in 1973.

After my operation I was put on a drug called digoxin to control and slow my heartbeat.

The drug worked very well, in fact at some point, too well. I can remember having to get up some nights to do sit ups just so I could feel my heartbeat.

On the other hand, after I'd played football or had an overactive night at Boys' Brigade, for example, I can remember sitting in a chair with my heartbeat racing and pounding away for hours.

At that time, I had no way of dealing with this powerful fast beat until I went to see a new Doctor at Southport Infirmary, when I was 21. He told me how to perform the Valsalva manoeuvre which involves holding your breath while crouching down to force a fast heartbeat to return to its normal rhythm.

This was a revelation to me and over the next 18 or so years I used this manoeuvre countless times after playing football, climbing up a hill, refereeing a football match, putting up tents at Boys' Brigade camp or if I bent down too quickly to pick something up.

The manoeuvre continued to help me live my life and control the fast, strong beats until 2004 when my heart started going fast doing everyday things like standing up too quickly, climbing stairs, and playing with my kids.

After a few stays in hospital, to control my heart via intravenous drugs, I was diagnosed with Wolff-Parkinson-White syndrome (WPW). This led to me having a catheter ablation procedure in October 2004 and I was amazed how such a "simple" short procedure could have such a massive effect on my life.

Very soon after having the procedure, my heart started to behave itself for the first time in my life, it started beating very quietly and the fast rates were a thing of the past – or so I thought.

It took me about a year to recover from the events in 2004, I occasionally had flutters or stronger beats but gradually they disappeared, and I started, with the help of my dog Kizzy, to grow fitter and more resilient.

By 2006 I was really starting to see the benefits of my "new" heart but as my confidence grew, so did my workload at work. I've always been very good at keeping the work/life balance in check but from 2010 to 2014, I became more preoccupied with work and it took over my life.

I was over-stretched, over-exposed, and, in some instances, out of my depth. In 2011/2012 I started retching and coughing every morning through the stress of a piece of work that has gone on to earn hundreds of thousands of pounds for the company I work for.

Thankfully, even though I was off work with stress for six weeks in 2012, my heart didn't show any signs of being affected. The stressful work didn't end there. In 2013 and 2014, I was involved in two more projects that just added to the build-up. All that was needed was a trigger.

That trigger came on the 11th of April 2014. I'd had a busy week. Besides work I'd done a brunch for Jake's trip to Thailand, got Sam to the airport for his trip to Iceland and visited the dentist for two fillings. While my mouth was numb, the dentist decided to tackle a third filling that wasn't necessary and while she was drilling, she caught and cut my gum.

I didn't think any more of it but the next day, while I was sat at my desk in work, my heart started to flutter. The flutter continued for the rest of the day, gradually getting worse as the day went on. I took myself to bed when I got home hoping to "sleep it off".

Unfortunately, it's very difficult to sleep when your heart is doing gymnastics in your chest, I was used to it pounding away in a rhythmical pattern, but this was different, this was very erratic. Missed beats, extra beats, faster beats, runs and stops.

I tried all the techniques to bring it under control but to no avail. All the time I was petrified that the cut to my gum had allowed an infection called endocarditis (an infection caused by dental treatment that slowly degrades your heart) to affect my heart.

I thought I'd need to go back into hospital to get it reverted back to normal rhythm but that filled me with dread so I kept giving it an extra five minutes and hoped it would stop. 36 hours later and with what felt like five different pulses beating away in my body (one in each arm, one in each leg and one in my chest) I was just about to give up and call an ambulance. I lay with my arms folded and said a little prayer.

This was at five to midnight on the 12th of April, by 12.05 I was lying in bed with a big smile on my face.

Somehow, and for whatever reason, my heart had return to its normal beat and it was beating as if the last 36 hours had never happened. My body started to recover, and I could feel the blood flowing back to my extremities.

Was it a miracle or a coincidence? I'll let you answer that question, but I know, as I lay there drifting off to sleep for the first time in two nights, that it felt incredibly Heavenly!

Since that lengthy attack, I've had a few less violent episodes (i.e. a 15 hour one in May 2014 and a few shorter ones). Now I'm in a much better place, I've removed as many triggers as I can from my life (i.e. caffeine and alcohol), I'm exercising as much and as moderately as I can and, after having a bit of an Epiphany a few weeks ago, I'm determined not to let work and the stress associated to affect me in such a deep and profound way as it has previously.

Enough is enough and I want my life back.

I feel incredibly fortunate and thankful to still be here, but I know how short life is and how it can change in a heartbeat.

The fight for that heartbeat goes on and to use another slogan from the British Heart Foundation – "It's Great to be Alive". Thanks for listening and never forget – Every Day Is a Bonus!

As she often does, Coco started barking at 5 a.m., obviously sensing danger. I got up, went to the loo and then gently reassured her that everything was ok.

When I got back into bed, my heart started flipping and flopping a bit, probably a delayed reaction from watching the first half of the football match last night.

Building on recent discoveries, I turned on the confidence tap and, as I'd done to Coco, reassured my heart that everything was ok.

And then I remembered what day it was and about the 36-hour bout of palpitations that had started on this day in 2014. Just for a second, and only a second, the doubt and anxiety crept in before reality took over and, like Coco, I drifted off to sleep until the milkman arrived!

The "fight for every heartbeat" mentioned in this post from 2015 still goes on but as the first lines of my current favourite song goes;

"For centuries, we have been at war, but this is where the battle ends… and I have won."

Have a great day everyone!

More Rounded

19th April 2018

The Final Word…

Yesterday and today I presented a short talk on Mental Health Awareness to my colleagues at work.

Last Saturday, while I was walking Coco through the sand dunes, I resolved that the talks would be the final step on my recovery that started over ten months ago with a visit to the company doctor.

A journey that has taken me through a whole gamut of emotions, exposed my vulnerability, challenged my anxiety, pushed me to the limits, revealed the extraordinary power of forgiveness, uncovered gaping chasms in society, brought deep-rooted fear to the surface, and instigated battles with deep-seated psychological issues. It has brought focus on missed opportunities, wasted years, lost fitness, and relinquished confidence; a multitude of negatives offset by a mass of positives, improved fitness, greater strength, increased understanding, heightened awareness, all-embracing tolerance, and a brand new me.

And now I'm here, still alive, bigger, better, more rounded, more able and finally the recovery from eight years of stress and anxiety-related problems is over.

Yes, I still want to reach the goal I agreed with my counsellor, yes I still want to go past that goal onto bigger and better things, yes I want to continue to grow and build on what I've achieved so far but for the moment, I feel complete!

And my heart is silent!

Thanks to everyone who supported me, pushed me, cajoled me, cared for me, loved me, and got me back to where I should be.

Enough!

X

Inspirational Children

22nd April 2018

Post from 22nd Apr 2017 - *Back home after another brilliant weekend in Kirkham.*

It's always inspirational to watch so many children in Boys' Brigade, each with their own individual challenges, overcome their difficulties and get along so well, in what could easily turn into a powder keg of emotions.

Yes, there were flash points, as there always is when you take a group of young people away, but enormous credit and thanks must go to the skilled, loyal, and dedicated volunteer leaders who give up their time and energy to ensure the children are looked after in a safe, loving, and Christian environment.

Special thanks go to Kay for the organisation she puts into the weekend, not just for the three days we are in Kirkham but also for weeks leading up to our time away.

Last year, I commented on how wonderful it was to see a first-time camper enjoying his time at camp despite his battle with homesickness. This year it was brilliant to see the same boy totally ensconced and at ease at camp and, sorry mum, he never missed home once! Another first timer got the camp bug too!

As for me, this weekend has completely freaked me out. Time and time again I would catch myself cruising through my "jobs" and activities without even a blink – and compared to the same tasks in previous years THAT was a revelation. It was also great to have in-depth conversations with other leaders about mental health while the sausages were sizzling! Roll on next year!

"Recovery is not linear, the path is not straight, obstacles will try to hinder your progress, darkness may engulf your mind, but you need to keep stepping mindfully into the light!"

"Don't just be remembered for the glasses you've emptied but also for the lives you've filled!"

May 2018

Everything's Changed

4th May 2018

I thought I had reached maximum freak out level, but this morning is in a whole new freaking stratosphere!

I'd become so used to exercising, even the flattest, shortest walk, getting home and feeling ok only for a couple of hours later, when the adrenaline had dissipated, for my heart to react with extra beats, runs and bouts of erratic heartbeats.

Getting to sleep would be very difficult as my mind would turn into a constant ECG monitor.

If I did manage to sleep, it would be very interrupted as the erratic beats and my mind's preoccupation would overpower any attempts to reach the required level of unconsciousness!

And then there's now.

Yesterday evening I literally took my exercise to a new level, hundreds of metres higher than I've climbed for nearly a decade and my amazing heart didn't even squeak.

I got back to my car and instead of prowling round for ages to try and stop my heart from reacting, last night I just sat down and drove home.

At home, I ate toast and cheese for supper, a definite "no no" after exercising in the past. I went straight to sleep, a deep, all-encompassing sleep only interrupted by Coco's frantic barking at 2.30 a.m.

When I usually get woken up so abruptly, my heart, brutally disturbed from its relaxed state, reacts, but not this time. And here I am out with Coco since 6.15. No palps, no ectopics, no weirdness, no anything, complete nothingness!

When my encouraging and amazingly strong friend, Kayleigh Crystal, shared her poem yesterday, for a second one part of the poem brought all those feelings of anxiety, stress, and total preoccupation right back with a vengeance! But only for a second as the other part of the poem washed them away like a stream washing clean a dirty pebble.

And that's it, all the work I've been doing challenging my anxiety, seeing the reality and gradually increasing the intensity of my exercise has washed me clean.

Given the speed and apparent "ease" of my recovery, some might question the severity of the problems in the first place. But it hasn't been easy or straightforward and there was a massive amount to overcome, correct, and rectify.

My desire to see all the positives, my need to escape the bonds placed on me by others, my focus on getting back to how I was in 2009 AND, dare I say, my Christian faith have got me where I am today, totally freaked out and clean. It is possible, all things are possible.

"I am a pebble on the riverbed, watching and aware, not caught in the stream!"

Opening the Conversation
8th May 2018

Last week, I posted about mental health awareness on the Company's Social Media platform, provided by Microsoft's Yammer.

Nearly 300 people from right across the business have read the post and it's encouraging that many have chosen to speak out, either publicly or privately, about their experiences. Many are relieved to have someone to speak to and that they no longer feel alone in their battles.

The post also instigated a chat with a fellow Christian who provides voluntary Pastoral Care in his spare time and wants to help promote greater understanding of mental health in the Company.

At the start of June, I'll be sharing my story to the Management Team and before that I hope to provide advice on mental health well-being to my colleagues.

It's happening, it's growing, it's time!

Breaking the Cycle

14th May 2018

Post from 14th May 2015:

After last week's battle of Scar Tissue + Virus against Sinus Rhythm, it's great to see that Sinus Rhythm was victorious. Thankfully, unlike last week when I had to think about every one of those 37 steps, the same doesn't apply this week!

You may have noticed that I've gone very quiet about my heart, it's bliss, isn't it?

Considering the progress I've made, sometimes I doubt how bad I was in the first place and I know that some others have had similar doubts.

It was encouraging to hear David Harewood, of Homeland fame, talking about his experiences of poor mental health this morning on BBC Breakfast. Hearing him say that it is possible to make a complete recovery from mental health problems really helped.

And then this post popped up on "On This Day" from two years ago when I'd been struck down by a virus which incapacitated me for a couple of days and further added to the anxiety/palpitation cycle that I was stuck in.

This post really reminded me how bad I was and how every day, sometimes every hour and every minute, were a constant battle, virus or no virus.

And here I am now, looking forward to climbing the final of the Yorkshire Three Peaks on Thursday, loving every second of my recovery and feeling a million times better than I did just a few months ago. The amazing thing is that for the last three weeks, I've been fighting another virus but because I've managed to free myself from the anxiety/palpitation cycle, my heart has not only not reacted but I've been able to do everything that I've done over the last two weeks.

When I was really struggling, I could see no way out and had almost given up hope but when I was heard, advised, directed, guided, and carried, I could start to heal.

I know it's not easy but if you are struggling at the moment, please try and find someone to talk to, please take steps to start that conversation and be heard.

A song which really helped me is Darkest Hour by Zakk Wylde (lead guitarist for Ozzy Osbourne), the guitar solo in the middle is massive and so are the lyrics.

"In your darkest hour, will you walk with me?"

Hope Sparked Into Life

17th May 2018

When the flame of hope sparked into life, as I climbed that sand dune on the 6th of October, I saw the chance to escape from the fear, anxiety, dread, and foreboding that had engulfed my life for so long.

Little by little, step by step, day by day, the spark became a flame and fuelled by forgiveness, focus, freedom, fortitude and, most importantly, faith, it became an inferno.

A 10,000-foot (2 x Pendle, 1 x Ingleborough, 1 x Pen-y-Ghent and 1 x Whernside) inferno.

This week is Mental Health Awareness week and I have read quite a few amazing stories of strength and resilience as hope replaced despair, confidence overcame fear and love conquered all.

Never give up, everything can change, the spark can return and burn very brightly!

#mentalhealthawareness.

Detached

22nd May 2018

If there was one word that could sum up the effects of poor mental health, it would be "detached".

I've written before about the cost of my struggles but, as I've finally managed to drag myself out of the all-encompassing black hole, began to stretch and be dazzled by the light that is now shining all around me, I realise how detached I've become from so many things.

The pre-occupation, the vicious circles, the endless anxious monitoring of each and every heartbeat, the ramblings and scramblings to understand my head and the effect on my Physical Health. All those have left me detached.

Detached from work. Tasks that I did while I was struggling that I don't remember completing or how I did them.

Detached from society and its lack of understanding for my predicament.

Detached from friends that I just didn't want to see or that I upset during my ramblings.

Detached from the basic hygienic care that we do without thinking. Flossing was the last thing on my mind.

Detached from exercise.

Detached from eating properly.

Detached from sleep.

Detached from my body.

Detached from my soul.

Detached from reality.

And as I dragged myself up into the light, the task of reattaching myself continues.

But it's not as easy as it sounds.

Every time you start to reattach to something that became loose, you revisit the feelings brought on by the remoteness.

Feelings that bring flashbacks and doubt and fear and loathing and anger and bitterness and, eventually, hopefully, thankfully, re-connection with what you've lost.

Time to suck it up and persevere!

Invisible Progress

29th May 2018

On Sunday night, as I lay down to sleep, my mind mischievously reminded me of how my heart USED to be when my head hit the pillow.

Even if I'd had a "good" heart day, with no noticeable problems and my confidence was raised, a number of ectopic beats were guaranteed as I tried to drift off to sleep.

Although benign, the extra beats would instantly raise my anxiety levels at a time that calm and peace were essential to achieve the deep, refreshing sleep that, at the time, my body craved.

But sleep was literally the last thing on my mind.

The anxiety would induce more ectopics which would be more severe, and sleep was overshadowed by the genuine fear of not waking up again. It was that stark.

As I listened to my mind on Sunday night, my attention naturally switched to my heartbeat and, even though I'd had two very busy days (including the match on Saturday night), my heart just purred quietly rhythmically and gorgeously.

I listened again last night, and the response was even more profound, more emotional and more powerful.

A lot of my progress has been very visible and very noticeable, but the realisations of the last two nights have a much deeper meaning.

Have a good day!

War on Mental Health

31st May 2018

I was made aware of the Wild Wellness Facebook page a few weeks ago and it provides invaluable help on a daily basis.

Today Nat, the creator of Wild Wellness, talks about the difficult times that are encountered on the journey to finding the light that may have become diminished in your life.

Many say the recovery from mental health issues is a fight but, as I've found out, it's not a single bout of conflict but a multi-battle, multi-layered and, in some cases, repetitive war that contains many steps, obstacles and distractions. Each of these have the power to either knock you off your stride or, in the worst case, take you back to square one and bring on greater, more severe mental health issues.

I've identified 16 different battles that I've encountered in my eight-year journey. Sixteen distinctive stages that are unique to my journey. They all differed in intensity and duration, but all could have had a drastic effect on my health, both mentally and physically.

Here are the battles, in chronological order –

Battle for survival

Battle for downtime

Battle for recognition

Battle for diagnosis

Battle for admission

Battle for support

Battle for innocence

Battle for acknowledgement

Battle for release

Battle for stability

Battle for fitness

Battle for calmness

Battle for peace

Battle for liberation

Battle for re-connection

Battle for closure

The chapters for my book, if I ever get around to writing it!

Spooky Encounter

31ˢᵗ May 2018

Another three hills completed on my recovery; Grit Fell, Brownley

Hill and Ward's Stone!

The walk was 10 miles and I only met one person on my way round, a lady jogging with her dog. I stopped to have a chat with Meg the sheepdog and the lady asked where I was going, and she said I was keen to be walking in the evening.

I explained that I was trying to get my fitness back after my battle with anxiety. Turns out she is a part-time farmer and a Cognitive Behavioural Therapist at Lancaster and Morecambe hospitals.

It was really nice to spend five minutes in the middle of nowhere talking about my counselling, my progress, and receiving her affirmation for the steps I'd taken.

A real boost and a very spooky encounter!

"Instead of allowing negativity to take things from your life, harness positivity to add more back!"

"May your smile accentuate your inner strength and beauty and not be a mask to hide the pain behind your eyes!"

"Choose to forgive but remember the pain that led you to make that decision and use it to prevent any future repetition!"

June 2018

Impromptu Moments

2nd June 2018

It's been an interesting few days.

My increased fitness levels have, as the counsellor predicted, allowed me to see many positives in the reality that had become hidden for so long and given a massive boost to my confidence.

This week, that confidence spilled over into my work, probably for the first time in five years, and showed in my design work and my contribution to meetings.

I've often talked about the damage my mental health issues have caused to my physical fitness but just think what I could have achieved at work if I had received proactive, timely, and effective support. The irony is not lost on me.

I can't talk more highly about my counselling sessions and, as I said to the counsellor, I randomly met in the peat bogs above Abbeystead on Thursday night, the counselling has literally changed and possibly saved my life.

Then yesterday there were two impromptu chats. In the first, my silence at certain moments said so much.

But the second one, over a burger and a pint, became deep, meaningful, and very enlightening. The person I was speaking to is on their own journey of recovery. A journey that has been long and difficult with many obstacles thrown in along the way. But they have reached an important point, the point of release and this will, hopefully, allow great progress to be made, in a similar way to my journey.

The chat answered many questions, shone a great light on many situations and has allowed our friendship to become even closer than before.

Impromptu meetings, interesting outcomes, mysterious ways!

Facing Demons

5th June 2018

I was up early to give Coco her morning "wee" walk around Staveley before taking her back to the house and driving up to Kentmere.

I'd spotted two more hills to climb yesterday, across the valley from Wansfell, but to get to Sallows and Sour Howes, I first had to challenge and conquer my demons.

At the end of May last year, I decided to try and walk the Kentmere Round, a 14-mile strenuous walk over nine hills. Even though I thought I was physically ready (although not as fit as I am now) my hidden, poor psychological health flared up as I took the first step up the initial incline. My heart physically reacted and although I managed to walk about a mile, the incessant extra beats that were driven by my anxiety, meant I had to abandon my walk before I even reached the foot of the first hill.

That was the start of my problems last year which led to a major flare up of years of anxiety that, although I thought I'd dealt with, were simply hiding, waiting for the opportunity to pounce.

Today, I faced those demons head on. I walked up the same path and reached the point that I failed at last time. Not only did I face my demons, I pushed them back, back over the cliff edge and as they fell to their death, I smiled, flicked the Vs and continued my walk up Sallows and across to Sour Howes. The Kentmere Round can wait for another day.

We all carry demons from previous experiences and failings, either because of our own limitations and poor health or because of other people's inadequacies. And we all have a choice how we respond to those demons.

Do we allow our anxiety to feed them, so they grow out of control and take over our lives?

Do we wallow in self-pity, sharing the demons around?

Do we take positive action to back up our words, do we face them, challenge them, push them back and destroy them?

The choice is ours. I can't stress enough the power of positivity in all this. It doesn't have to be walking up a hill, it can be recognising the simple beauty in an everyday blessing, understanding and helping others and giving your time to support someone else.

Demons hate positives, they hate being challenged, they hate being pushed back, they hate cliff edges, they hate being laughed at and they hate you taking back control.

I'm loving seeing things from a slightly different angle!

Don't Compare
14th June 2018

Each mental health illness is unique to the individual person and it's impossible to compare the difficulties faced by one mental health sufferer to the next.

Every case has a different background, different duration, different cause, different triggers, different symptoms, different recovery techniques, different recovery times, and different outcomes.

Even though fellow patients may be able to empathise with each other's experiences, it's virtually impossible to fully understand the devastating effects that the other person is having to face on a day-to-day, hour-to-hour, minute-to-minute basis.

Since I opened up the conversation at work, and had many powerful, informative, and enlightening chats with friends, it has become very apparent that no two mental health cases can be compared.

Some may be short term, others lifelong.

Some very traumatic, others appear easier.

Some find an effective resolution, others fail at every turn.

Some have difficult starts and easier happier ever afters,

Some straightforward beginnings and complex endings.

Some find it difficult to share, others reveal all their secrets.

Some leave lasting damage, others total repair.

All are unique, difficult and individual, encompassing an infinite combination of challenges.

Although none can be compared, those that suffer can find solace in others who face similar struggles. Sharing experiences, motivating, advising, cajoling, encouraging, sharing, understanding, supporting and, most importantly of all, listening.

It's not a race or competition to see who can cross the line first but how many of us can reach a positive resolution and who we can help along the way.

All different, stronger together.

Noticeable Reactions

18th June 2018

Since Coco started wearing a muzzle, it's noticeable the reaction that it brings from other people. I've noticed the looks many times but none more so than when we came down from Wansfell into Ambleside last week.

A mixture of fear, uncertainty, disgust, and disdain was etched on faces as we made our way through the streets, but the main look was one of guilt.

In their eyes Coco is guilty, no questions asked, no need for discussion, no need for explanation, no need for evidence.

It was nice today, as we waited for our bacon butty at the Squirrel Cafe in Freshfield, to have a chance to speak to a man who was waiting with his Akita. He got it. He understood. He listened. He even praised Coco for standing up for herself.

But Coco's predicament highlights something else that I've really discovered recently, it's the truth in the age old saying, "Don't judge a book by its cover!"

Don't judge a dog by its muzzle, don't judge a person by their appearance, don't judge someone's actions without first understanding what they are going through.

Coco is such an inspiration to me. The way she deals with situations especially given the constraints that have been placed on her by the incompetence of others. The way she battles her anxiety. The way she still shows love and care and trust to those who need it.

I owe her so much.

Some people will never "get it" but thankfully, there are those that do!

And the bacon tasted all the sweeter after our chat!

Riding the Storm

18th June 2018

It may seem trivial, but it felt good to get the all clear at my six monthly dental check-up this morning but that's only part of the story.

I also took the opportunity to confirm something that I'd read on the Internet about stress causing inflammation of the gums, which can be misdiagnosed as Gingivitis leading to expensive, painful, and exhausting deep cleans.

It was enlightening to hear my dentist's response.

Another side-effect of the excessive levels of stress compounded by the lack of dental hygiene, that was the last thing on my mind when I was preoccupied by my heart. Poor dental hygiene that has led to intense, expensive, and challenging treatment over the last few years.

And then, probably because I was feeling anxious about my check-up, my heart started to flip and flop this morning while I was in bed and, for the first time in six months, my Delta Wave was active.

But, and here are the positives, not only did that give me another chance to use my anxiety control techniques (for the umpteenth time) which increased my confidence level even further, it also reminded me just how bad I did feel when I was struggling, that I wasn't imagining it all and that I could control it.

The biggest positive though was the fact that although I wouldn't arrive at work until 11, I didn't take the easy option and work from home. That would have been a retrograde step and, even though my heart was a little mischievous throughout the day, and that brought back many difficult memories, I rode the storm and made it through, proving how bad I must have been when I did work from home in the past.

Following on from yesterday's excellent healing service at Church when the emphasis wasn't on "I can walk" or "I can see" experiences but on becoming whole, at peace and as one with yourself, today is another step closer to being totally healed!

And the beauty of that type of healing is, it's not just available to the select Church going few, but everyone!

Onwards and upwards!

Value of Sharing

19th June 2018

I've been struggling for some time about how much I share on Facebook about my recovery from my mental health issues.

I don't want to appear to brag.

I don't want to make it out that it's been easy.

I don't want people to get sick of hearing about it.

I don't want fellow strugglers to feel downhearted or disillusioned.

But I do know the value of sharing experiences and know, firsthand, that it has helped others far more than a "cut and paste" chain post which does nothing more than trivialise the situation.

And then this post appeared on a group for Wolff-Parkinson-White sufferers yesterday.

"My family think this heart disease is nothing except my son and partner, so I think I'll leave the group because it's all in my head!"

A desperate post where the poster is throwing in the towel due to a lack of understanding of her heart condition because her family don't understand it. And because there are no outward signs, they've never experienced it and never suffered from it, it doesn't exist and it's all in this poor girl's head.

This post is about an invisible, sometimes undetectable and difficult to diagnose syndrome, very similar to mental health issues.

The response to this post from members of the group has been simple. "If you've never experienced the effects of WPW, then you'll never understand it".

The only way to change the views on invisible illnesses, like WPW and mental health, is for those that have experience in the conditions to talk about it, share their experiences and hopefully save people, like this poster, from "throwing in the towel".

And the only way that society is going to take mental health issues more seriously is through education provided by those who've suffered and struggled and discovered and hopefully recovered!

Beauty All Around

21st June 2018

You accepted the decision

Understood the reason

Rationalised your reaction

Deflected the dejection

Strived for realisation

Rebuffed the rejection

Now you feel your heart's pace

Listen to your mind's peace

See the beauty all around

Noticed nature's love abound

Rediscover the real you

Re-centre your holistic view

And suck it up and persevere! :-)

Time to Change

22nd June 2018

Post from 22nd June 2015"

Living with a heart arrhythmia is a constant battle between trying not to listen to every heartbeat and being ready for the next out of sync beat that could lead to days of palpitations.

It affects your confidence, your speech, your ability to do even the simplest of tasks, what you can eat, what you can drink, where you can walk, and your inner self. But it teaches you the preciousness and fragility of life, and how important it is to live every moment and be eternally grateful that, thanks to God-given talents of very skilled Doctors, you are still here to enjoy life

I am incredibly thankful and at this moment my heart is beating like a dream! :-)

Today I saw a drawing that perfectly captures the haunting battle between the mind and the psychosomatic effects aggravated by the conflict.

As well as illustrating the anxiety-palpitation cycle, it also encapsulates the all-encompassing fear of your own heart, with its potentially deadly arrhythmic beats, and the constant anguish of not being able to speak out through lack of confidence and worry about subsequent discrimination, isolation, and misunderstanding, which would lead to increased turmoil.

Talking about your situation is the last thing you want to do but, as my recovery demonstrates, it's the most important thing to do.

On the 27th of June 2017, I was invited to a "welfare check" with HR.

The check was in response to the previous six-week flare up of anxiety that I'd experienced due to factors outside of work.

During the meeting I was handed a leaflet for a free counselling service and told to sort out my own counselling.

The last thing I wanted to do was pick up a phone and talk to an invisible stranger about my problems.

I was also referred to the company doctor who, unbeknown to me, had been available since before 2008. Dr Andrews encouraged me to talk about everything and the seven-year battle finally came to light.

The cat was put amongst the pigeons, who appeared startled even though they knew exactly why the cat was so angry.

If only I'd been given the opportunity to speak, to someone who listened, sooner.

Then the drawing wouldn't be so haunting!

Time to change. Speak out. It's ok not to feel ok.

When you are heard you can start to heal.

The Further I Walk

25th June 2018

The further I walk,

 The higher I climb

The quicker I recover

The more I discover....

What an ignorant, insensitive, indiscriminate, intolerable, destructive, demeaning, deadly, demonic, frustrating, frightening, fractious, frantic, time-wasting, life-changing, brain-damaging, soul-destroying little shit that anxiety is and don't let anyone tell you different.

The further I walk

The higher I climb

The quicker I recover

The more I discover

That it can be defeated!

"The lines on my face are the contours of the hills I've had to climb!"

"In this world there are people who will those that succeed to fail because they fail to have the will to succeed!"

"Never miss an opportunity to experience the simple joy of riding your bike through a massive puddle with your feet off the pedals!"

July 2018

Victory in Sight

13th July 2018

Post from 13th July 2017:

For the first time in ages, it feels amazing, if a little weird, to wake up and not be able to feel my heartbeat! I should dream about making fish posters more often!

Thankfully, over the last year, this feeling, of not feeling my heartbeat when I wake up, has become a daily occurrence.

I'm incredibly proud of all the steps I've taken to make that possible and so glad I didn't wait for that improbable help to be forthcoming.

Here's a little ditty I wrote a few days ago"

"Couldn't wait for you, had to push through

You paid no heed to every plead

Waited an age for you to engage

Choosing to forgive in order to live

Life at a haste, no more to waste

A waiting game, guilt in pain

Onward I go, stronger I grow

Higher I climb, reclaiming my prime

Victory in sight, love and light!"

Have a peaceful day everyone!

Don't Compare

22nd July 2018

Comparing people's individual experiences of mental illness, is like comparing a grape, an apple, an orange, and a coconut. They are all fruit, but all germinate, grow, and harvest differently.

One is squashed very easily, one has a soft outer skin that shows the inner bruises, the other's harder exteriors that keep the signs of damage inside.

Two don't need to be peeled to reveal their inner secrets, the other two need to be peeled and even broken.

But all four need care, all are good to share, all are fragile, all release beauty when encouraged to open up, and all desire to be loved.

Notice their blemishes and harvest their spirit. Don't compare, share, reveal, peel, and help break the stigma before the devastating rot sets in.

Contrasts

23rd July 2018

Post from 23rd July 2016:

I couldn't decide where to walk today, along the side of Derwentwater and up Catbells or round the Lake and up Walla Crag.

To most walkers Catbells and Walla are like a walk in the park but for me they can be a big challenge. It's taken some time and a lot of trial and error, but I've learned to listen to my body and let it decide my limits.

Even though I might not scale the heights of others I can still discover the beauty that lies within my limits and for that I'm eternally grateful!

Learn to love your limits, they are yours and yours alone.

Embrace where they take you, worship what they show you.

Believe in what they tell you.

They are not a burden to hold you down but a path to a life for you to own.

On this day two years ago, the fear that gripped my heart prevented me from even attempting to walk up Catbells and Walla Crag. The contrast between then and my current challenge is clear to see.

The main drivers behind the change were positive thinking, demonstrating to my mind through step by step evidence that it was telling me lies and rebuilding my damaged confidence.

Positivity > Negativity.

 Confidence > Fear

Causey Pike > Catbells

Keep stepping!

Open and Honest

28th July 2018

On Thursday, my new friend Rebecca Worthington posted this status on her very inspirational and informative Facebook page called TeamReb.

I'm trying to make a difference. I want to be a role model. Someone that you can use as an example when starting conversations about mental health and illness. I never imagined I would be in this position when I first began experiencing symptoms of depression. I write and speak about all aspects of my life in the hope it will help others feel less alone.

As an advocate I've began experiencing this strange notion. A notion in which I have to be ok. To be okay and have it all together, all the time. I've got an audience now, and I'm feeling a pressure (that I've put on myself) to always 'be strong', for fear that others may give up or lose hope.

In reality this isn't what recovery is like though.

To show depression and recovery in its true form I must be willing to be more open and present myself on both the good and bad days. I've decided that I don't have to be fully well to make a change. To say that I'm doing well all the time would be lying, and as a society we are programmed into showing only the best bits, posting pictures of only our happy moments. But as someone on a journey of recovery with a depressive disorder, I think we need to see more honesty.

I need to practice what I preach and learn to not be ok all the time, to be more open, to break down, to show weakness and to show how I feel. You don't have to 'stay strong,' you have to be authentic, that's what's inspirational and that's what will get people talking about this topic.

In the post Rebecca talks about how she struggles to appear to be "ok" and strong all the time to prevent others from losing hope in their battles with their mental illnesses.

Rebecca's paragraph about being more open and honest about difficulties we all face in our battles really hit home with me.

I commented on the post that during my battle I'd always wait until I had recovered from my difficult situations before I posted because I didn't want others worrying about me and I felt the need to always appear positive to help others that may read my statuses.

But that approach has a major drawback in that it makes it appear that my battle is easy and that I simply shrug off the difficult times.

Something that I know is far from the truth.

So, I have decided to be more honest too and to highlight the negatives and the challenges more openly and to talk about them sooner.

Here goes.

Today was very similar to the day in October when I took my first step in challenging my anxiety.

As happened on that day, this morning I woke up with my heart on edge and beating slightly out of sync.

As happened on that day in October, I took Coco for a walk in the Pinewoods.

As happened on that day in October, by the time I started walking my heart was stable again and I set off over the sand dunes towards the beach.

The wind on the beach today was also similar to the wind on an October day and I walked headlong into it.

But that's where the similarities between that October day and today ended.

In October, I was unaware of the devastating power of mental illness on my physical health, today, however, nine months later I was able to apply everything I've discovered since to ensure that not only was my heart ok during the walk but I could control, through calmness and relaxation, how it recovered after I left the beach.

The walk could have pushed me back to the day before that October day. It could have shattered my confidence that I have built up climbing the peaks on my challenge. It could have led to a long bout of palpitations later in the day.

But it didn't and by controlling my anxiety that in the past had caused so many problems, my confidence has actually increased today.

It could have been so different but thankfully, the lessons I have learnt, the advice I was given by the counsellor and the support I've received from so many people helped me through today and, like the day in October, it feels amazing!

Thanks, TeamReb!

"Respect is not bought by power, position, or possession but earned through time, tenacity, and tenderness!"

"Even desolation looks beautiful in the sunshine."

"Pay attention to the quiet ones, by their very nature they choose their words more carefully."

August 2018

Listening to my Body

11th August 2018

I had plans to drive up to the Lakes this morning and climb a few more peaks for my challenge.

The weather had improved, my heart was settled, and I was feeling good.

Then last night my heart started to flutter, an early warning sign of a bug working its way through my heart, I didn't sleep well and woke up with a high temperature and cough.

The reality was far from glamorous. I was disappointed, frustrated, and even thought about ignoring my body and pressing on regardless.

And then the honesty kicked in.

The combination of a bug and my heart is a challenge, add to that heat and inclines and the danger level increases but throw in anxiety and tension (from worrying about how my heart would react) and the cocktail becomes explosive.

The main thing I've learnt from my battle with anxiety-driven palpitations over the last five years is to listen to my body, show common sense (thanks Mum and Dad), be honest with myself and, even if it is frustrating, to rest when necessary.

So, I went to my second favourite place instead, the beach!

Clearer Thinking

15th August 2018

If I was to write a book about my experiences of mental illness, this would be my final chapter.

So, Holiday Club was just for the kids, right?

So, we could teach them about God, life, friendship, fellowship, and love, right?

Yeah that's right, but Holiday Club also taught me a lot about myself, where I've been, how bad I was, how I've recovered and how I've started to rediscover the real me.

When I was asked to tell the story on the Thursday, I struggled to think of the right level, the right approach and the right words to get the message across. Then one morning, I woke up and my brain had formulated a plan.

Over the next few weeks I tinkered with the approach until I was happy with the format. But even on the morning of the talk, I was altering things slightly until I was happy.

The story went well, and the message was shared but that was only part of the teaching.

I realised that I'd rediscovered the adaptability that had been missing since 2009.

For the first time in nearly eight years, my mind was free to work through things, to concentrate on things, to mull things over and resolve things.

This change, although invisible and probably unnoticed by others, was very evident to me.

My mind that had been preoccupied for so long with anxiety, fear of palpitations, uncertainty, and lack of focus, was suddenly thinking more clearly, and I was able to express my thoughts in a more coherent, logical and rational way.

I always shy away from using the "D" word when I talk about my struggles. I was never diagnosed with depression and I feel that it is bandied around too frequently in society with little thought to the connotations that are associated with such a powerful and devastating word.

But even though I was never formally diagnosed with depression, as I've started to feel better, I've realised that I was either very close to full blown depression or I was actually in the depths of its hideous grip.

I've heard many people compare depression to being in a black hole and I can certainly empathise with the analogy.

What might start off as a feeling of being lost and alone in a shallow dark place can soon exacerbate into a much deeper, darker and all-encompassing feeling of complete doom and despair.

If you get chance to realise that you are falling into that black hole, you may start to desperately scramble your way out but as the sides of the hole are like dust and the base of the hole like soft sand, your struggling just ends up dragging you deeper and deeper into the chasm below.

The deeper you descend, the blacker your view becomes, and your visual horizon is continually reduced until you can just see flickerings of movement over your head as your desperate pleas for help become inaudible to those that pass by.

You become invisible, alone, isolated, insular, fearful, and depressed.

Unable to escape the hole, you become disconnected from your friends, your family, and society in general.

Even if the blackness relents for a short time, the sheer exhaustion of the battle just to survive and the embarrassment of your invisible predicament, means that socialising, even with your closest friends, becomes a major challenge. A challenge that you can't face and instead you prefer to spend time alone in what has now become the safety of your black hole.

As time goes on you become more detached, more isolated, more unable to reengage, more preoccupied with your struggle, less focused, more exhausted, deeper and blacker with a narrower view of the world around you.

You wait, you fight, you scramble, you wait, you sleep.

You try, you hurt, you scream internally, you wait, you sleep.

You force yourself out of bed, you wait, you sleep.

You wait, you sleep.

Friends will try to reach you, they attempt to pull you up from your hole, to lift you and reconnect with you but you just want to stay where you are safe, alone.

You try, you wait, you sleep.

Some people will give up on you, misunderstand you, misinterpret your actions. They will ignore you, belittle you, disown you.

You hurt, you wait, you sleep.

You see people who have the power to save you, who have the tools to lift you and support you, who can change things, who should understand, who should come to your aid. Their lack of engagement enrages you; it frustrates you, you resent them for their lack of action. You try to attract their attention, but your protestations fall on deaf, unresponsive ears and the anger, the bitterness, and the blackness becomes deeper.

Then after years of turmoil there's a glint of hope, a chance, an opportunity but with that comes a greater fear of misunderstanding, of further rejection, of greater darkness.

You try, you talk, you hope.

They hear, they understand, they diagnose, they direct, they encourage, they listen.

You take the first steps on your recovery. You start to feel more settled, slightly stronger, more ready for the fight.

Those in power finally offer some support, they lower a rope for you to pull yourself up. But the rope is covered in grease.

Two feet up, one foot down.

You persevere, the light becomes brighter, you become stronger as you pull against the slippery rope.

Two feet up, one foot down.

Your increased confidence allows you to expose deficiencies, rattle cages, ruffle feathers.

Two feet up, one foot down.

You near the lip of the hole, invigorated by your progress.

Stones rain down from above.

Your cage rattling, your cats amongst the pigeons has stirred up resentment and exposed guilt.

The stones crash against your head, they dent your body, they crash to the floor of your hole.

More stones rain down as they try to silence your stories and damage your progress. The base of the hole is covered, the stones deep enough to stand on.

You use the stable ground created by the stones as a foundation to stand on, a force to push against and you continue your ascent.

Two feet up, three feet up, four feet up, five feet up.

The stones continue to rain, you continue to climb, faster, stronger, more resilient.

Then you reach the light, your hands let go of the rope and grip the lip of the hole and you push with all your newly found strength out of the hole and into the world.

The light hits you like a laser beam, you unfurl, you stretch, you blink, you fall exhausted but free.

You rise, you step, you walk, you climb, you grow, you live, stronger, more rounded, more focused, more able, more adaptable, more you.

Breathing space. More aware, more ready, more able to fight the next fight.

The Thursday story at Holiday Club? It was all about spreading good news...

Stay strong, keep reaching, keep unfurling, keep stepping, keep growing.

Notice those around you, spot the changes, reach out, lay stones for them to stand on, lift and support.

Turning Point

17th August 2018

August the 16th 2017, a year ago yesterday, was a turning point on my recovery.

I was due to have a telephone follow-up call with the company doctor, who diagnosed my mental illness, so he could check that I was ok and that the actions he'd recommended were being carried out.

I was ready to tell him that I was progressing well but there hadn't been much progress on the other fronts.

An hour and a half before the call I was told, during an impromptu chat, that there was little likelihood of a response to my struggles and that the recommendations may not be actioned.

I had a decision to make, either offload over the phone or employ selfish forgiveness.

I chose the latter and at that moment, everything changed.

I look back on that day with fondness as it marks a line in the sand and I've used it as a safety net a few times, that I can fall into if things flare up again.

Interestingly, yesterday, I had another similar battle with my mind which caused me to fall into the net, but I immediately bounced back and continued on my journey.

And then, just before I left for home for my holiday, someone approached me about continuing the mental health conversation at work.

Firstly though, I'm off to Devon for a bit!

I Can't Resist

23rd August 2018

When my inner alarm clock woke me at seven o'clock, for a split second, I thought about turning over and dozing off again. Then this King's X lyric popped into my head …

"I can't resist, I couldn't see how this could be an accident. I can't resist, I want to see more."

I've done all the walks from the cottage, so I drove the couple of miles to Brownstone Car Park just outside, the superbly named, Boohey.

The plan was to walk down to the South West Coast path and along to Coleton Fishacre, the National Trust garden in the cove.

What an amazing walk.

The contrast between the natural unspoilt beauty of the cliffs and the man-made World War II Brownstone Battery (another lasting reminder) was plain to see. But without one, we may not be here to be able to marvel at the other.

The randomness of the cliffs and naturally dense woodland gave way to the manicured gardens and palm trees of Coleton Fishacre before I headed back to the car.

And then, slap bang in the middle of a farmer's field I spotted the Daymark, a 25-metre navigational aid built in the 1860s – well worth going the extra mile.

I'm so glad I didn't resist!

Inspirational Story

23rd August 2018

I don't read many books. I'll occasionally see one that grabs my attention, buy it, read the first few pages and then lose interest.

In July, I just happened to be driving when I caught the end of an interview on Radio Merseyside with someone called Andy Grant.

I sat in the car outside my house, transfixed by his story, his battle to rebuild his life after losing a leg in Afghanistan and the mental illness that followed.

He was on the radio to talk about his book that highlights his experiences and recovery from physical and mental illness. He wanted his book to be an inspiration to others.

I found Andy on Facebook and recognised him from LFC TV. He mentioned on his Facebook page that I could order a signed book from him. I messaged him and shared a bit of my story. The book arrived three days later with an encouraging message inside the front cover.

I couldn't put the book down; his story is very inspirational.

No two mental health situations are the same and it's important that you don't compare your situations or recovery to that of others. But there are parallels to be drawn. There is hope to be gleaned. There are questions that can be answered.

Quite a few situations in the book really hit home with me but several lines in the penultimate chapter rang true with my current situation.

I've f**king done it! I thought as my heart swelled with pride. I've proved to everyone I can do it. All those hours were worthwhile – all the turning the cage with the screws, learning to walk, the hours between the parallel bars, the amputation, the infections. The months of pain and misery and heartache and disappointment were worth it. Whatever happens for the rest of my life, no one can take this from me.

I've put to bed Andy the Injured Soldier. I'll never start a presentation or a conversation in the pub about Afghanistan, or about getting blown up.

I'm Andy Grant and I'm the fastest one-legged man in the world, I would tell them.

Don't ever define me by a trip wire, by war, by a moment of pure chance that saw me blown to pieces. Don't ever define me as being disabled, as being a former Marine.

The tables had turned.

That is how I felt when I sat looking at sea this morning.

Andy's book is called "You'll never walk" because the last word of the Liverpool tattoo on his damaged leg was removed when he had his leg amputated. He proved that wrong!

Inspirational!

In the Driving Seat

24th August 2018

Back home after a lovely family holiday in Devon. The "lads" may be a few years older, but we crammed in as much as we used to do when we went to Haven or Farmer Peter's in the early years of the 21st Century.

Trains, boats, crazy golf, bike rides, card and board games, crabbing, loads of laughs and leg pulling (of a slightly more adult variety) and battlefield live with a group of Call of Duty hardened eight- to eleven-year olds.

Before the week, as there weren't any peaks over 450 m nearby, I decided that I'd use the holiday to try and regain my fitness that had lapsed since my last Lake District walk six weeks ago.

All the walks were amazing, different, and challenging in their own way, especially walking the ups and downs of the South West Coast path. By the end of the week, I feel that my fitness and confidence have returned to their previous levels.

But there was one moment that stood out as a major turning point.

When I went for a walk on the first evening, I climbed up the path near the cottage and headed down to the banks of the River Dart. As I reached the lowest point, literally, my heart began to throw extra beats and it felt like it was going to develop into full blown palpitations that could have seriously affected the rest of the week.

I felt stranded, alone, and anxious.

The only way back to the road was to climb back up the slope from the estuary.

Compared to the walks I've done before, the incline was slight, but the anxiety had dented my confidence. Then the newly found mental fitness kicked in, I recognised the effects of the anxiety, quelled the tension, pushed the fear away, and started to slowly walk up the slope.

The first few steps were filled with trepidation, then my heart got the message from my brain that everything was ok, and it responded in kind and smoothly switched into "walking mode".

That moment set the mood for the rest of the week, allowing me to see the sights that were dazzling all around me and enjoy the rest of the week's activities with my family.

The roller coaster of mental illness continues but that moment demonstrated that I'm in the driving seat now and more able to control the ride!

Onwards and upwards!

Choosing Wisely

25th August 2018

Post from 25th August 2015:

People who think anxiety is JUST a state of mind have never truly suffered from this terrible disabling disease.

Anxiety can start for many reasons.

You become anxious about your job, your family, your friends, the world, your finances, your future, your health and although it may originate in your head if it's not dealt with at the earliest opportunity it starts to affect your wellbeing until it eats away at your muscles, your bones, your organs, right down to your very core.

The deeper it goes the more your health, your work, your finances, your family and your friends suffer which leads to more anxiety and the cycle goes on - deeper and deeper.

Like a lot of things in life it is very easy to let it destroy your life but incredibly difficult to free your mind and body from its grasp.

I've mentioned a few times about the last five or six years of my life and looking back I've realised how badly anxiety has affected me, not only my heart with its many and varied types of palpitation but also other areas of my life.

And only now, by putting processes in place to help me recover, I've started to free myself from its grasp.

My weight loss and exercise have both worked to reduce the stress on my heart which has led to my body being able to deal with situations that arise with less anxiety and therefore allow my body to heal.

But also, I've realised that subconsciously and consciously I've changed my

139

approach to things that occur which help deal with frustration, regain control and reduce anxiety.

Fate is a great mate and the other day Facebook served up this great quote which sums up perfectly how to handle situations that are thrown at me.

"I chose to live by choice, not by chance; to make changes, not excuses; to be motivated, not manipulated; to be useful, not used; to excel, not compete; I choose self-esteem, not self-pity. I choose to listen to my inner voice, not the random opinions of others. I choose to be me."

These are not barriers or defences to protect me, but the blood of life itself ... my blood, my life.

I really hope this helps other people suffering with anxiety and stress. I have found typing this status very cathartic.

There's one more to add, "I choose to forgive not to blame" and by doing so I free myself from the shackles that may burden me.

Three years on from this status, I wasn't aware then, that I was just at half time.

Life is full of choices.

Our choices can help or damage our lives or the lives of others.

In the past three years, and especially the last year, the choices made by others have had a dramatic and devastating effect on my life.

Do you choose to engage or ignore?

Do you choose to forgive or bare a grudge?

Do you choose to stand tall or cower in fear?

Do you choose to support or frustrate?

Do you choose to move on or allow it to fester?

Do you choose to be proud or to shrink?

Do you choose to release the chains or carry the burdens?

Do you choose to carry on with your life or watch time go by?

Do you choose to be you or to be changed by them?

Choose wisely!

Perseverance

31st August 2018

Mental illness will try every trick in the book to knock you back, even trying to turn positives in your life into negatives in your head.

But when it realises you've sussed it out and are on its case, it scurries away, like every type of bully, back into the shadows.

And every time it hides it becomes a bit weaker and you become a bit stronger, more ready for when it tries to attack again.

Recognise, react, repel, repair, rally, resolve.

Persevere.

"You only truly appreciate life's beauty when you've experienced its fragility."

"Who knows what the future will hold but time and patience are the best pain healers, problem solvers and true feeling revealers in the world … use them to your heart's content!"

September 2018

Too much awareness

2nd September 2018

We all know that increased awareness of a subject is a good thing, right? Especially when it's awareness of a debilitating, often invisible, illness.

But is too much awareness a good or a bad thing?

Before I was diagnosed with stress-induced anxiety, as I wasn't aware of the underlying cause, I just put it down as one of those things that life throws at you. After all, I'd already spent the vast majority of my life living with an undiagnosed heart syndrome and just carried on the best I could before I became aware of Wolff-Parkinson-White syndrome.

After both diagnoses my awareness of each subject grew immensely through research, sharing experiences with others and recognising the effects.

Last Wednesday, I celebrated two anniversaries, my 26th Wedding Anniversary and the first anniversary of my all clear from the cardiologist. Late on Wednesday night I posted about my progress since that all clear but early on Thursday morning, I decided to delete the post.

I deleted the post because I was aware of the upset that my celebration could bring to others that may be struggling with similar symptoms or challenges.

I felt happy that I'd deleted the post but also frustrated because I hoped that as well as celebrating my progress, I wanted others to benefit from my experiences.

Thursday was one of those days and because I am more aware of mental illness, I knew that was the cause. I knew I was giving out signs that I was struggling, but no one could see them. This led to increased frustration and worsening symptoms.

Then on Friday morning, because of my awareness, I sussed it out. My mental illness was trying to trick me. I was on to it. I could see it. I could feel it. I could dismiss it. I gave it a label: it!

Turns out it was behind everything bad that had been happening.

It was behind the strange thoughts, the cravings, the desires, the misunderstandings, the misinterpretations, the lack of engagement, the lack of understanding, the lack of support, the blame, the bitterness, the anger, the frustration, the resentment, the tension, and the loneliness.

It was the driver of the random roller coaster, it built the track, it strapped me in my seat, it enjoyed the ride. A veritable little it, with a silent and invisible "sh" in front.

When it strikes, we have a choice how we respond.

Do we run away from it?

Stay away from the places and situations where it knows it can affect us?

Do we hide from it?

Do we cower from it?

Do we let it control us?

Do we let it take over and ruin our lives?

Or, as my counsellor advised, do we face it? Stand up to it? Go where it lives? Go where it thrives? Do we challenge it? Give it the opportunity to attack? Do we fight it? Push it? Shove it? Do we make sure it doesn't control our lives? Not let it ruin our future? Do we do all we can to defeat it?

If it triggers physical symptoms, it knows that by making you react will help it to thrive, to grow, and to make those symptoms worse so it can flourish. But by not reacting, by not becoming tense and anxious, it isn't able to initiate the cycle that it craves.

As I drove into work, the place where it resides, knowing I'd exposed it for what it is, a smile came across my face. I could visualise it running away to hide. It was cowering. It had lost control. It couldn't take over. It couldn't ruin. It was weak.

I was strong, I could go where it was, I was more aware, it was nowhere!

All About Balance

10th September 2018

Naturally, over the last few weeks, I've been thinking back to this time last year and remembering the situation I was in.

I recall every day being a struggle as I prepared myself for my first counselling session, because of this my anxiety levels were high and I would sit at my desk, slap bang in the middle of my office, just getting through each day.

My feelings of anger, resentment, frustration, and despair must have been etched across my face and very evident in my demeanour but because my predicament wasn't public, understandably, no-one noticed.

My renowned productivity, motivation, and desire were at an all-time low and even the positivity of the cardiology report hadn't registered, such was the deep-rooted fear of my own heart.

The counselling would change all that. It would change me. It would change my future. Settle my mind. Help me deal with those devastating feelings. Reinforce my choice of reaction. Teach me techniques that I could use to quell any future attacks, either from my heart, mind or, when they both work in tandem, the cyclic effect of both.

All that would lead me to today, able to look back, compare and recognise the changes. To see that the negative, destructive, un-Christian feelings have been dealt with through forgiveness and the positive attributes have returned.

Things have changed at work. Instead of being left to tread water and simply see out my days, I've been listened to, heard, supported, stretched in an achievable way, and given responsibility that has changed my demeanour and allowed me to regain the traits that had been so badly damaged.

All very positive.

But because I'm getting used to my heart being quiet again, I notice every little foible, every little run, every ectopic and every change of pace, all explainable but still disconcerting.

Last night was the perfect example. I'd done a bit of weeding and cut the grass but nothing too strenuous. Kay, Sam, and Kate were out, and I was relaxing watching telly when I felt my heart suddenly pick up speed and beat loudly like it used to do.

There was no reasonable explanation but instead of becoming tense and reacting, as I would have done pre-counselling, I applied my techniques and, the best I could, let it have a jog through the night.

This morning I worked out the cause. Something delicious that I'd enjoyed for my tea was having a party in my hearty!

From the psychological side, as expected, triggers pop up that try to resurrect those negatives.

Unexpected, difficult to look at, hard-to-swallow posts remind me of why things were so bad at work and test my resolve to continue to apply those techniques and not react, not inflame, not escalate whilst needing to highlight failings in a subtle, anonymous, non-confrontational way.

Given my experiences and discoveries, I'm really looking forward to what I can glean from, and possibly share at, the Heart and Mind, Body and Soul festival, in aid of Heartbeat on Saturday.

It's all about balance.

Vagus Nerve

15th September 2018

It was encouraging to hear the speakers at the Heartbeat festival today. Nice to hear and meet Rebecca Worthington from TeamReb, to listen to former Super League Referee Ian Smith, to hear the haunting song about a girl who had committed suicide in Preston Marina on Christmas Eve and the raw poem by a lady who had found the strength to write about the abuse she suffered as a child.

All the talks further emphasised the uniqueness of everyone's battle with mental illness and the steps they have taken to control and overcome the debilitating effects that it brings.

During the last session, by a serving Police Officer who provides mental health support and education in Lancashire Constabulary, he mentioned the power of the Vagus Nerve and being able to control your nervous system during times of stress.

It was during this talk that I shared my experiences of the Vagus Nerve and how I used it to control the Supra Ventricular Tachycardia with the Valsalva Manoeuvre. It dawned on me that because I'd been so used to controlling my heart by literally forcing its beat back to normal for nearly twenty years, that was how I tried to control my heartbeat while it was being fuelled by anxiety.

The change came when my counsellor gave me a new technique which encouraged me to actually welcome the discomfort of the palpitations and, instead of forcing the Vagus Nerve to be an internal defibrillator, to encourage it to relax and let my heart return to its normal beat naturally.

Life-changing and life-saving advice, that literally changed and possibly saved my life!

Six Words

20th September 2018

In the six hours that I spent with my counsellor, during September and October last year, I don't remember him speaking very much. He was too busy performing miracles in a less vocal way.

He did something that had been sadly lacking in my situation until that point, something much more powerful than idle chatter. He listened. He heard. He directed. He advised. He challenged.

Some people speak so much but say so little, others speak so little but say so much.

At the first session, the week before, I had offloaded everything, passed on my written evidence of my seven years of struggle and he took a few notes.

Before the second session he had assimilated my situation, applied his professional skills, mapped out my path, and was ready to utter a short six-word sentence that would change my life.

"You need to challenge your anxiety!"

I was filled with dread, and initially that sentence made things worse, he was filled with confidence, as if he already knew the outcome.

He knew that if I could challenge my anxiety, head on, my heart would settle.

He knew that when my heart had settled, the really battle with my head could commence.

He knew that battle would expose the anger, the resentment, the frustration, the bitterness, and the disappointment that was fuelling and driving my struggles.

He knew that by exposing those negative thoughts, the positivity would return.

He knew that with the positivity, the confidence, the focus, the motivation, and the perseverance would follow suit.

I don't know how he knew, but he knew.

I remember being in awe of my Auntie Bett.

She'd sit in a smoke-filled room with my amazing nan and Auntie Madge in full Scouse flow.

Auntie Bett would sit and listen, then, in her beautiful Scottish voice, she'd utter six words, cut to the chase and everyone would fall about laughing thanks to her wonderfully humorous insight.

She knew she had that power and so did my counsellor.

Six words!

"I am here, if you need!"

Scepticism Apprehended

21st September 2018

I've used the mindfulness technique, many times, including last night when my heart started flicking slightly in my sleep.

When I first heard the technique, I was very sceptical about how it could even touch my physical reaction. I fully understand why and how it works now and it's not just for controlling your heartbeat.

Pain or discomfort leads to tension, preoccupation and the body's natural reaction against the pain – triggering the "fight or flight" response from the Vagus Nerve.

The technique asks for the pain and discomfort to actually be welcomed into your body, which hopefully reduces the tension and preoccupation and stimulates the "rest and digest" or "tend and be-friend" response from the, now legendary, Vagus Nerve.

Although the Vagus Nerve can't treat the underlying reason for the pain and discomfort, by altering the way you react and staying as relaxed as possible, the effects of the pain will hopefully reduce, the associated anxiety subside and confidence increase.

Unexpected Setback

30th September 2018

I love having a life-long, very close relationship with my heart. We've been through so much together.

I can tell when it is having a bad day, having a moment or, as in recent months, when it's happy and settled.

Given its history, I've become very aware of its every move and I often get pre-occupied with its idiosyncrasies. Recently though, I've reduced the monitoring and dimmed my awareness as my heart has been very well behaved, quiet, and unnoticeable.

As I drove to Malham yesterday, after a couple of hours at work, I could feel my heart triggering a few ectopic beats.

Ectopic beats are difficult to ignore as they feel like something is randomly punching your heart from the inside. As I've had a break from the ectopics for a few months, I noticed this latest batch even more.

The effect of these beats is not just to temporarily disturb the conductivity of your heart, it also brings your heart's functionality back into focus. Once your mind is aware of the change in your heart's beat, it is difficult to ignore and the more you think about it, the more it adversely reacts. The ectopics become more frequent leading to longer runs, disturbances, and palpitations.

Between 2013 and 2017, the ectopics were triggered by the anxiety. The ectopics brought on the pre-occupation. The pre-occupation instigated tension, adrenaline, and a "fight or flight" response. The tension increased the anxiety which in turn activated more ectopics and the cycle went on and on, sometimes for days.

As I set off on my walk, the ectopic beats subsided but as I started to climb, they returned and a battle between my mind's memories of those four years of pain and the lessons I've learnt during my recovery commenced.

If this situation had occurred before September 2017, my "fight or flight" tension-filled response would have caused the attack to take hold, I'd have had to shorten my walk, the journey home would have been difficult, I'd have been very quiet for the rest of the evening, my sleep would have been very disturbed and the following day would have been full of aftershocks.

My response yesterday was different and based on the techniques and advice provided by my counsellor and discoveries that I've made over the last 12 months.

While I stood looking over the limestone-covered valley that surrounds Malham, instead of instructing my Vagus Nerve to instigate a fight against the ectopics, I concentrated on my breathing.

Breathing in kindness and understanding and breathing out resistance and tension.

As has happened on many occasion before, the attack gradually subsided and I was able to carry on my walk, albeit more gingerly as my confidence had been dented, see the positives in the actions, drive home safely, enjoy the second half of the football, chat to Kay about my day and hers, sleep well, run up and down the stairs several times at Church this morning to get the TVs working before the service and enjoy a lovely meal with Kay and my amazing mum, dad, Auntie Barbara and Uncle Dave.

I refer to the ectopics as a "Delta Wave". It's probably not the right medical term but as the Delta Wave is a small triangle in my ECG trace and the tell-tale sign of Wolff-Parkinson-White Syndrome, I can visualise it and that makes it easier to understand and deal with.

The same goes with the change in approach to the Vagus Nerve, instead of seeing it as an aggressive enemy, I now see it as a calming friend.

I've no doubt that the Delta Wave and ectopics will continue to appear as and when the triggers occur, and my reaction will be tested again in the future but the positives from yesterday's negative experience stand me in good stead to come out smiling again next time.

So much changed during this week last year, things that I will probably never talk about publicly, but the changes changed everything!

"Love is ...
Doing something for your partner without being –
Asked,
Nagged or
Expecting something in return!"

"It's easy to make a simple life look complicated, the real skill lies in making a complicated life look simple!"

"There are enough hours in the day, it all depends on how you choose to use them."

October 2018

A Pivotal Moment

3rd October 2018

Post from 3rd October 2017: *It's Coco time! :-)*

For the previous four and a half years, almost every night after work had been "Coco Time" but, on this night last year, Coco's welcome home was extra significant.

Events that occurred during the day had threatened to take me down an impasse; a path of conflict, deadlock, and disagreement. An unwanted direction that would hamper, if not derail, my progress, undo all the brilliant work that my counsellor had instigated and increase the severity of my suffering.

A pivotal moment, and I didn't have a clue what to do.

The answer came at 2.30 a.m. the next morning as a familiar voice spoke to me and woke me from my fitful sleep.

Amidst all the turmoil in my mind, the voice had calmly assessed the situation, analysed the possibilities, weighed up the outcomes, and decided on an approach to what lay ahead.

As instructed, I got my phone, went to the loo and as everyone else was sleeping, I typed up the voice's plan so I could formalise it later that morning.

The plan?

A different path, a surprise approach, a deconfliction, a recovery of control and, unbeknown to me at the time, a sight of closure.

"Coco Time" is always one of the best times of the day, even more so on that day. DoG really does work in mysterious ways!

Raising Awareness

10th October 2018

Looking back as I've recovered over the last year, I've recognised that even though my mental illness silently built up over time, there were major changes in my personality and demeanour that an aware and trained eye could have spotted and, as with a physical illness or injury, if support had been provided the mental illness could have been dealt with earlier.

Early identification would have prevented the illness burrowing deeper into my inner self, causing the eventual physical reactions and preventing the exhausting recovery that I have endured.

As today is World Mental Health Day, it's the perfect opportunity to raise awareness of mental health and highlight the need to be more aware of other people in your family or circle of friends and to recognise any changes in their demeanour that may signal that they are struggling mentally.

By raising awareness, the stigma that surrounds mental health is reduced which, in turn, hopefully makes it easier to initiate the conversation, highlight if further support is required and action to be taken.

But this vigilance should not just be for a single day each year, but we need to be aware every day.

If a person close to you is becoming increasingly irritable, distant, insular, forgetful, pre-occupied, easily angered, struggling to sleep, losing trust in others and confidence in themselves, unable to concentrate and possibly feeling trapped, check up on them and start the conversation.

Time to Change are currently running an "ask twice" campaign to encourage us to not only ask friends, that we are concerned about, how they are, but to follow their response up with a second question, "Are you really ok?" and that might open-up the conversation and allow them to share their concerns.

Time to Change offer five simple steps for when someone opens up about their mental health –

1. Take it seriously

It can feel embarrassing and exposing to talk about your thoughts and feelings, especially if they're disturbing. Don't laugh or treat it like a joke. However strange it might seem to you, remember it's real to them.

2. Listen and reflect

You don't have to have all the answers – just listening can make a big difference. Try and show that you're taking on board what they're saying. You can do this by reflecting – that is, saying something simple like "that sounds really difficult". You could also say something like "thanks for telling me", to show that you appreciate having the conversation.

3. Ask questions

We worry about prying when it comes to others' mental health, but it's better to ask questions. It can help them to get things off their chest, and by keeping the conversation going it shows that you care.

Some of the questions you might ask:

"What does it feel like?"

"What kind of thoughts are you having?"

"How can I help?

4. Don't try and fix it

It's human nature to want to fix things but expecting things to change right away isn't helpful. It's not your job to make their mental health problem go away – it's often more helpful just to listen, ask open questions and do things you'd normally do together.

5. Build your knowledge

You might find it helpful to learn a bit more about what they're going through. If they mention a specific diagnosis, you could learn more about it and read personal stories by people who have experienced similar things.

You might want to learn about the professional help that's available to them and suggest that they explore those options. *Mind* have a handy guide on seeking help for a mental health problem, and *Rethink Mental Illness* have advice on what to do in a crisis.

Together we can change how mental illness is viewed in society and by recognising the signs possibly save someone from serious consequences and long-term illness.

Hoping for Normality

16th October 2018

A lot of our young people have their own individual challenges and they expend a lot of energy trying to deal and live with their difficulties. They may be anxious about their time at school, have many unanswerable questions constantly whizzing through their minds and never really have the chance just to be themselves and just be a normal young person.

During their time with us, at Church or Boys' Brigade, it is important that they have some time of normality, some time away from the questions and investigations and a chance to express themselves in their own individual way, while we still maintain the traditions of discipline that underpin the organisations.

Mindfulness is an amazingly powerful gift, but overuse could lead to a mindful-mess when all you want to do is get back to normality and feel a bit of mindfulless instead.

It's all about finding the right balance.

Something to think about, but not too much!

Everyday Triggers
17th October 2018

I've mentioned before that when you are dealing with mental health issues, it's almost impossible to avoid everyday triggers that try to resurrect those negatives feelings associated with mental illness. And that we need to be aware of the potential attacks and try to have mechanisms in place to recognise and deal with the threat.

Yesterday, through a National Trust video, of all things, the little $#IT tried and almost succeeded in dragging me back down that path.

While watching the video, and seeing how two hard-working Police Officers deal with the stress and anxiety that comes with their job while also running a young family, I felt a complete failure that I'd not been strong enough to withstand what I'd been through and the little $#IT tried to pounce on my reaction.

Thankfully, I recognised the attacker from previous encounters and was able to fend it off by remembering that every mental health situation is different, everyone's thresholds for dealing with mental health situations are unique to themselves, everyone's background is their own and that there is no embarrassment or failure in not being able to do things that others find easier.

Apart from that, it was a really nice, uplifting video!

Understanding Others

23rd October 2018

Although I hate what I've been through, I love how it has changed me by raising my awareness of the feelings of others whilst also being able to keep a lid on how I react to their challenges and negativity.

My experiences have also helped me understand how the children that I work with at Church have to deal with their individual challenges and I find their reactions easier to understand and help mitigate.

It has also allowed a number of powerful and encouraging conversations to take place, when others have felt safe to share their stories with me, and I'm able to offer my support and help them to progress down their path whilst continuing on mine.

Now I have more control of my reactions, I'm also able to deal with the frustrations that the inadequacies of others used to trigger in me.

"When we drift from a place of love, kindness, wholeness and forgiveness, we feel "out of sorts" and often express bad energy (anger, fear, complaining, etc)."

My battles between my diagnosis in July 2017 and July 2018, in a nutshell!

Goal Reached, Challenge Completed

27th October 2018

I'd been planning today for some time but, following my struggles in Malham only four weeks ago and the minor palpitations I'd experienced this week from a bug, I was very nervous about how my heart would react to such a strenuous walk as the Kentmere Round.

Thankfully my heart brought its "A" game to the fells today and while we walked the fourteen miles, over ten peaks, climbing over 4,000 feet, while being buffeted by 50 mph gusts in -12 wind chill, my heart didn't even squeak. No extra beats. No palpitations. No flutters after we'd finished. No reaction while my tea was digested.

We've stayed at Ghyll Bank in Staveley more than thirty times over fifteen years and I've always wanted to walk the Kentmere Round but either the weather or my health prevented me from even attempting it.

In May 2017, I tried and failed to even reach the base of the first peak and that, together with other incidents, caused a major flare up of anxiety and led to my diagnosis of a mental illness in July 2017.

I agreed with my counsellor that, to challenge my anxiety, my goal was to complete the Kentmere Round.

The ten peaks we visited today not only allowed me to reach my goal but also completed my forty-five peaks over 450m challenge for Heartbeat.

And it was also an amazing way to celebrate the fourteenth anniversary of my catheter ablation in 2004.

Thanks to Clare and Paul Singleton for their support, company, and numerous breaks today.

Well done to Kay for completing the walk and thanks for all her support over the last several difficult years.

Thanks to Dr Hamilton, Dr Todd, Dr Andrews, and Dr Laraway for the surgical and psychological skill.

And thanks to everyone who has been there for me and has so generously donated to Heartbeat, spurring me on to complete my challenge.

The Little "It"

28th October 2018

Anxiety, stress, and grief are invasive, invisible, silent, and very difficult to identify. Their effects are misunderstood, traumatic, disabling, life-changing, and, in the most extreme situations, tragic.

They can trigger devastating symptoms and exacerbate pre-existing physical illnesses.

When my counsellor advised me to "challenge my anxiety", he told me that by reaching our agreed goal, not only would my confidence return but he predicted that my anxiety would be completely defeated.

As I've progressed from walking up a sand dune in October 2017 to reaching thirty-five peaks, before this weekend, I've gradually prepared myself for the final goal and decisive battle with my anxiety.

I've referred to my anxiety as "it". This allowed me to visualise it, focus on it, push it, challenge it, make it run, make it hide, give it some of its own medicine, making it shake with fear, and eventually destroy it.

The only problem was that my anxiety knew the final battle loomed, its destruction was at hand and, on the run up to the final assault, it would use every trick in the book.

It needed to reduce my confidence. That happened in Malham when even the slightest incline caused my heart to react, increasing the fear of intense climbs on the Kentmere Round.

It needed to try and prove I was weak. That happened on Thursday when my heart fluttered after doing some physical work while I was staving off a bug.

It needed to demonstrate that my heart was susceptible. That happened on Friday after I experienced a short bout of palpitations after climbing a short incline and eating my lunch.

It needed to put me on edge and increase the tension as close to the final assault as possible. That happened after we did a short walk from the cottage down to the village and back up the hill on the Friday. The walk went well, but, as the evening went on, my heart started beating stronger and more noticeably, bringing my heartbeat into my mind's focus and disturbing my sleep.

It thought it had the upper hand. But it had forgotten the techniques I now possessed and its attempts to thwart my victory simply gave me more opportunities to prove that I was still in control.

Every attack was quelled.

Every disturbance was settled.

Every charge was stopped, and I knew I was still in control of it.

Instead of my confidence being damaged, it increased.

Yesterday's walk was more than the end of my challenge for Heartbeat, it was more than the final step towards my goal.

Every step I took, every foot of ascent, every break to successfully recover, every peak, every suppressed concern, every palpitation-free minute, every piece of positivity dealt a devastating blow to the anxiety and victory over the little "it".

Challenge your anxiety, recognise the positives, try to take control, surround yourself with loving and supportive people and take steps to defeat this insidious, unseen, and aggressive enemy.

"Be generous with your giving and frugal with your taking."

"Hindsight is a wonderful thing; it allows us to piece together the events that explain the person we are today."

*"Be the King of the town that you own,
Noone else has the right to sit on your throne."*

*"Do. Lead. Support. Help. Make.
Try to reach your highest possible target,
It may make you easier to be shot at,
But everyone needs someone to look up to!"*

November 2018

True Friendship

3rd November 2018

Around this time last week, we were about to set off on a walk that would change so many things.

I'd already changed a lot but the next eight hours, fourteen miles, and ten peaks that lay ahead of us would take me further on my journey of recovery and discovery than the previous eighteen months, one hundred miles, and thirty-five peaks.

Given the challenging run up to last week's walk, I firmly believe that without the support of the three friends who accompanied me on the walk, I would have failed to complete the walk, failed to reach my goal, and most likely failed to complete my challenge for Heartbeat.

I'd walked most of my previous peaks on my own and, although I'm very adept at talking to myself, as I completed those walks, I was constantly monitoring my heart.

Waiting for the next strange beat.

Waiting for the reaction.

On guard.

Tense.

But last week was different, even though the walk was a lot more strenuous than I'd done before, because I spent the walk catching up, laughing, joking, sharing stories and experiences with my good friends, I didn't even notice my heart.

The anxiety that had tried and tried to derail my attempt didn't get a look in. I was able to put down my guard and the post-walk tension didn't get the chance to grow.

But that's only half the story.

Before randomly bumping into Paul outside the chippy in March, I hadn't seen or spoken to him for years. When I bumped into him, I mentioned about my goal and, being a very experienced mountain walker, he offered his time and support for the Kentmere Round.

Last Saturday, as we met up in Staveley and, considering the time that had passed since we'd met Clare, we all just clicked as if we'd just seen each other the day before. And, together with Kay, the time, love, and support we shared as good friends helped make a challenging experience even more memorable and I'm extremely thankful for that.

Time may pass, distance may grow, and circumstances may change but true friendships never end!

Remembrance

5th November 2018

I've been trying to put into words the feelings I experienced, from my unique view, at the NHS Memorial Service yesterday.

"As I stood atop the balcony, looking down at those below.

I witnessed all their dark, transformed into a glow

Tears were shed, stories shared, love embraced, smiles exchanged.

Candles were lit, ribbons draped, memories recalled, flowers placed.

Loving glances, sensitive words, comfort found, all around.

Calm ensued from chaotic thoughts, some very fresh, others profound.

From my almost heavenly view, a sense of ethereal kind,

That they are not gone but live on in your heart and mind." ♥

Just a Smile

10th November 2018

When just a thought, a memory, a moment in time is enough to induce a smile; it's the most beautifully simple yet powerfully evocative smile of all.

No text, no voice, no post, no glance, no meet, no greet required; just a thought, just a memory, just a moment in time, just a glow, just a warmth, just a light, just a smile!

Shine a Light

13th November 2018

There have been many pivotal moments in the last year of my recovery –

The diagnosis

The positive cardiology check-up

Being advised to "challenge my anxiety"

Seeing the reality

Choosing to forgive

Successfully using the breathing technique to quell the palpitations

Conquering the sand dune and staying relaxed

Walking up Pendle Hill, my first peak over 450m

Completing the Kentmere Round

But this status was also pivotal, as events on this day last year answered so many questions. But because of steps I'd taken up to this point, my response in this status speaks volumes …

Post from 13th November 2017:

When someone finally shines a light on their poor handling of your past, use it to illuminate their failings rather than cast a shadow on your successes. Malarkey!

… and the word malarkey, sums things up perfectly!

Medicinal Disparity

21st November 2018

There is a disparity between how medication is viewed for physical and mental illnesses, increasing the stigma that surrounds the latter.

Taking medication for heart disease, arthritis, viruses, and other physical illnesses is not seen as being weak but, probably due to lack of understanding, harnessing the power of medication for mental illness is seen as shameful, feeble, and, in some cases, desperate.

Correctly prescribed treatments can have dramatic life-changing effects or by "turning the volume down" can provide breathing space to allow initial steps to be taken on the road to recovery.

Given the guilt that envelops a mental illness, the bravery to take any positive step should be admired, supported, and encouraged.

Winning Hand

23rd November 2018

Post from 23rd November 2017:

Take control, sit, wait, seize your opportunities, stand your ground and don't be intimidated!

It's probably a good sign that I can't remember what happened on this day last year, to trigger that post.

Maybe another foiled attempt to push me off my path, another drop on my roller coaster recovery ride or another victory in my fight to be me again.

Whatever it was …

I had all the winning cards in my hand,

the strength, the truth, the power to stand

I could've damaged reputations,

I could've changed perceptions,

But too many tears had already been shed,

So I chose to keep the evidence inside my head!

… and my confidence grew …

"I'm here for a reason and just lost focus I'm learning how to counter your attacks you talk to me I'm talking back" ~ Harley Poe

"Even if you don't talk to a friend very often, you can still show them how much you care. Just be in the background so if they need you, they know you'll be there."

"It's not about self, but the wealth you impart on others."

"Appreciate the unnoticed before they notice they're unappreciated."

December 2018

Worth Every Penny

3rd December 2018

Today was the last payment of the vet bills for the treatment of the dog that attacked Coco in October last year.

When I arrived home from the Magistrates Court, last February, after accepting Coco's life-long Control Order and removing the Destruction Order that was hanging over her, I was under no legal obligation to pay the other owner's vet's bills. So, when the letter was pushed through my letterbox, with impeccable timing on the same day, I had a decision to make.

Ignore the bills and not repay them.

Repay them in full in a single payment.

Repay them in instalments.

I may be perceived as being weak, but I decided to repay the bills in instalments.

I couldn't afford to pay the bills in full in a single payment and if I'd refused to pay, the other owner would have taken further action against me and, after just getting control of my life back from my mental health problems, I wasn't prepared to let someone who couldn't control their dog to have control of my life.

The letter I wrote confirming my decision gave me the opportunity to take back control and by paying in instalments forced the other owner to make sure that a similar incident didn't happen again and Coco would, hopefully, be safe from another attack.

Yes, it cost me x pounds but knowing that I was not being held to ransom, not being put through more stress, more court appearances and solicitor visits, knowing that I was in total control of the situation by demonstrating my strength and, most importantly, that Coco was safe was worth every penny!

Safety Nets

10th December 2018

Recently, I've been wondering how certain people can deal with excessive levels of stress while others can't.

We all have different levels of physical strength; some can complete triathlons while others struggle to walk round the block. Physical strength plays a part in dealing with stressful situations, but I think there is more to the required resilience than physical endurance.

For a variety of reasons, everyone lives busy and challenging lives, but when you are left exposed with minimal support facing situations that fill you with trepidation, the fear of failure takes things to a completely different level.

Moving to a new house, facing financial uncertainty, grief, divorce or single parenting, places all the burden, all the decisions, and all the difficulties on an individual's shoulders.

The fear of failure overshadows everything, all their choices, all their thoughts, all their conversations and all their life.

The anxiety that the fear induces exacerbates the levels of stress and further complicates your situation.

Feeling unable to handle stressful situations when others seemingly take it in their strides also increases the feelings of inadequacy and failure.

Eventually, without any intervention or support from others, the body physically reacts to the mental anguish and the dread morphs into a life-changing monster that causes a dramatic escalation of the problems, bringing the fear of failure to life itself.

All the difficulties, all the turmoil, all the pre-occupation causes noticeable changes in personality, increased isolation and debilitating loneliness leading to a dramatic reduction in confidence which allows the anxiety to intensify the downward spiral of despair and instigate the anxiety-physical reaction cycle.

The fear of failure was instrumental in my mental illness, both before the physical reaction from my heart in 2013 when I was fearful of failure in work and after the physical reaction when I was fearful of failure of my heart and the devastating resulting consequences.

On Saturday, when I realised the importance of the fear of failure in my situation, I viewed it as a major moment in my journey and it explained the reason behind why I couldn't deal with the excessive levels of stress like other people can.

The Facebook memory this morning brought into focus exactly how many years of my life had been affected by the mental illness and how things would have been different if more awareness had been in place to recognise and act on my difficulties earlier. As I've mentioned before, this then triggered a reoccurrence of the anger, resentment and frustration that I managed to deal with earlier in the year and I could start to feel the grip of anxiety begin to tighten in my body.

I knew the cause and I had to find a way to deal with it before it spiralled out of control again.

As I walked down the canal at lunchtime, I randomly turned around to look back down the towpath and in the distance the distinctive shape of Pendle Hill shone in the sunshine. Suddenly, as I remembered reaching its summit, a smile returned to my face and I could feel the anxiety gradually release and dissipate.

Once you've been affected by a mental illness, the memories and experiences never leave your brain and it waits for the trigger. Any trigger.

Self-recognition, awareness, and techniques can help repel the attacks and, as Pendle Hill proved today, having memories of achievements and progress can be used as a safety net to bounce off when the ominous grip of your mental illness tries to take control again.

Impromptu Situations

15th December 2018

It always amazes me how impromptu, random situations can develop into profound and meaningful conversations in unexpected places.

When I arrived at the bacon butty van this morning a man I'd met before, who owns an Akita and understands Coco's issues, was waiting for his coffee but the coffee maker was being fixed so I went for another short walk around the pinewoods.

When we arrived back at the van, the same man was still there but he was talking to a man who had arrived while I was away.

While I was waiting for my bacon to be fried, the conversation between the three of us drifted to illnesses and the Akita owner mentioned that he suffered with musculoskeletal which took an age to diagnose and he had struggled to find medicine to relieve the symptoms.

He then joked that the best thing he took was Kalms which he only knew about from when his wife was pregnant, but it helped bring calm to his mind, reset his sleep pattern, and slowly he started to feel better.

The conversation then turned to the power of the mind, how he can't sleep in the back bedroom because it reminds him of his illness, how I relearnt to accept that my heart would go fast when I exercised, how he and his friend cope with PTSD from their times in the army, how he still struggles to sleep and how Coco helped me to keep going when I could have just sat and vegged.

By now his wife had left to walk home, my brew had gone cold, and an impatient Coco had tried, thankfully unsuccessfully, to grab my bacon butty.

On the outside, the Akita man always appears in control, well-balanced, and self-assured but our conversation demonstrated again that the hidden inner life experiences paint a different story.

Hopefully our conversation helped.

"Until you talk, listen and understand, you'll never see!"

Emphasising With Others

22nd December 2018

For obvious reasons, I can't fully appreciate how difficult it is to live with Premenstrual Dysphoric Disorder (PMDD), but I can emphasise with the feeling of having your life fall apart.

When I was really struggling it was every day with no respite but, as I've gradually dealt with the anxiety that engulfed my life, the struggle has eased but I still get days when my heart will react and everything becomes a real challenge again.

It mentions, in an article about PMDD, that "women can feel like they're losing their minds, can't control their emotions, can't be productive, can't be around their partner. The loss of control is significant enough that it makes some women suicidal" and that is exactly how I felt, and occasionally feel now, when my heart has "one of those days".

Thankfully, unlike PMDD, my bad days are less frequent. It must be horrendous to have those symptoms on a regular and frequent basis, and the same goes for people living with Fibromyalgia etc.

Physical triggers of mental illness that are misunderstood by society, probably because of their invisibility, but nevertheless, as real, damaging, and disabling as a broken leg or a heart attack.

I'd never heard of PMDD until a friend told me about it.

Their struggles are real, their strength incredible, and their lives inspirational!

Finite Time

25th December 2018

There's something different about walking the dog on Christmas Day.

The roads are quieter, there's a smell of food being prepared, and sprouts being charged, the sound of Marshside Brass Band echoes round the streets and, occasionally, a child wobbles and weebles along the pavement on their new bike.

I've just been thinking how this Christmas Day walk would have been if things had taken a different course at the Magistrates Court in February, and Coco wouldn't be here to walk with me and our time together would have been cut, unjustly, short.

Christmas is a joyous time, when families get together and celebrate the most precious gifts of all; love, joy, peace, patience, kindness, goodness, gentleness, and, most importantly, time.

Unfortunately, in today's troubled world, the only one of these things that we can be absolutely certain about is time and how finite it is.

Thankfully, me and Coco can continue to enjoy our time together, but others aren't as fortunate and their losses are felt more painfully on this particular day.

Share sometime today to reach out to those near to you who are struggling because of grief, loss, pain, illness, loneliness, isolation, anxiety, or depression.

A short text, simple small talk, a warm handshake or a loving hug can make a massive difference to someone who is silently pleading for someone to give them just a second of their time.

Happy Christmas everybody!

Masking Difficulties

27th December 2018

It's not just easier to explain, you may not realise that it's anything other than a physical symptom.

Coughing and retching for weeks in 2012. The return of the palpitations while sat at my desk during a stressful time in 2013. The thirty-six-hour bout with the fear of endocarditis after dental treatment in 2014. Multiple days of extra beats and out of sync rhythm in 2015 and the constant fear of my heart's functionality in 2016.

It took till 2017 for an experienced and understanding eye to see past the physical reactions and diagnose the mental illness that was fuelling everything.

That moment started to change my view on the power of mental illness, increased my awareness of its devastating power, and helped me understand how some of the things the children in Boys' Brigade said might be hiding something more challenging.

Be prepared to look past the physical symptom that may be masking the real difficulties someone is facing!

Similar Paths

30th December 2018

I've mentioned before about how Coco has inspired me during our time together.

Our journeys, over the last thirteen months in particular, have followed similar paths because of very different situations that were forced upon us.

Both situations could have resulted in serious, even deadly, consequences and, in November 2017, we were both blamed simply for defending ourselves after the failings of others.

Shortly after the dog tried to attack Coco, and recognising the clinical ferocity that Coco used to defend herself, we decided that to "protect" her from future instances of self-defence, she'd always be muzzled, especially in the local neighbourhood. We felt that was sufficient action that would allow us flexibility in other areas.

When the permanent and life-long control order was imposed in February I was worried about how Coco would react.

Putting a muzzle on a dog with a nervous disposition and instantly taking away her only real form of self-defence could have seriously damaged her confidence on her walks.

At times, when she senses danger, she'll refuse to walk out of the drive, other times, like this morning, she'll just want to keep on walking and refuse to turn around!

It's been mentioned that a lot of dog owners faced with a control order have their dog euthanized voluntarily, in some cases, to save the inconvenience of having to make allowances for a permanently tethered and muzzled dog.

To give in and end Coco's life through no fault of her own would have been the wrong end to her story.

In a similar way, if I'd continued to tread water and be written off following my mental health problems, if I'd not spoken out and removed the invisible muzzle, and if, with help from Coco, I'd not regained my confidence, 2018 would have been a completely different year.

Thanks Coco!

Hopes and Dreams
31st December 2018

At this time of year, we look forward to what the new year may bring.

We have hopes, dreams, and goals but, unfortunately, the only thing we have real control over is how we choose to respond to situations that might not align to our plans for the approaching twelve months.

This time last year I was looking forward to 2018.

I had hopes and dreams and I was halfway towards a goal that I'd set with my counsellor. We had agreed that the goal would bring greater stability to my heart, reducing the fear which still existed, that in turn would bring peace to my anxious mind and clarity on my future.

But those plans could not foresee that I would be summoned to court to fight for Coco's life, that the fourth step towards my goal would be hampered by three inches of snow and that work would undergo a major organisational transformation that put jobs at risk and for a period brought greater uncertainty to the workplace.

I couldn't change the course of the civil charge that had been taken out against me, but I could proactively agree to a control order and remove the threat of the destruction order.

I couldn't stop the snow from falling but I could use my time in Staveley to improve my fitness and practice my breathing technique when my heart reacted, increasing my confidence even further.

I couldn't stand in the way of the restructure at work, but I could work with the new managers, be positive, and realise the benefits that the long overdue changes would bring.

Accepting negative situations and transforming them into positive experiences.

Positivity that would lead me to randomly bump into someone who, together with his wife and Kay, would provide invaluable support as I reached my goal; to allow me to climb Ingleborough on the 45th Anniversary of my hole-in-the-heart operation, honouring the amazing skill of my surgeon, Dr Hamilton; to complete my challenge for Heartbeat; to talk about my mental health problems at work and at Church; to finally reach my goal; to rekindle a friendship with a great friend.

Life will always throw problems at us. By accepting that fact and learning how to respond correctly to the problems won't stop things going wrong in the future but it will make us better equipped to deal with future situations and reduce their impact on our lives.

Happy New Year; take control of your 2019!

"People may think they are well off, but you are only truly rich when you give away everything for the fulfilment of others."

"Sometimes even unconditional love needs a bit of conditioning."

January 2019

New Year Wish

1st January 2019

In this new year …

May troubles be few, your friends be true, and life serve up a tasty brew.

May love last long, your heart be strong, and the radio play your favourite song.

May peace surround, simple life astound, and laughter shared with all around!

Small Steps

11th January 2019

When you are battling a mental illness or recovering from a physical injury or illness, it's perfectly natural to feel overwhelmed or daunted when you think about reengaging with a world that may have left you behind.

Reconnecting, emerging from your imposed safety/comfort zone and proving yourself again, can feel like massive, impossible, and frightening strides into the unknown.

When your confidence has been destroyed and your reputation damaged, the fear that overpowers your mind and the size of the challenges that lie ahead make standing still feel safer, easier and your only option.

Taking small steps forward, at your pace and in a comfortable secure direction, with friendly support, will change your view.

Small steps reduce the chance of failure, gradually increase your confidence and the impact of any problems that occur can be limited by marking your progress with quiet celebration that builds a buffer to cushion any expected stumbles.

As your self-assurance increases, your steps become more positive, your outlook brighter and the once unreachable strides begin to appear accessible.

Small steps, gradual growth, positive progress …

Keep stepping!

Your Choice

17th January 2019

Post from 17th January 2017:

Choosing to be you is one of the biggest, bravest, and bestest decisions you can make.

You will never leave you.

You know you best.

You can talk to you like you've never been apart.

You can meet up with you whenever and wherever you want without raising suspicion

You are never alone when you are with you.

You get you, while others might not.

You glow for others to see.

Hey you, be you!

For whoever is struggling with things at the moment –

There are moments in your life when people will bombard you, they will test you, they will attack you, they will blame you, they will anger you, they will push you into a corner, they will try to provoke you into retaliation.

You struggle to figure out your response, you can't react, you can't fight back, you can't shout out, you can't push back.

They want to destroy you, they want to punish you, they want to trip you up and catch you out, but you have a reaction that they cannot damage.

The decision to continue to be the innocent, beautiful, and loving you and the power you have to resist their ill thought through instant reaction and inconsiderate agenda.

The choice is yours to not let them change the you that you are.

Rely on the friends that are around you, fall on the love that surrounds you and have confidence in the strength that your battles have built.

Moments will pass, you will always be you!

Society's Misconceptions

21ˢᵗ January 2019

There's a misconception of how mental illness affects people; "…mentally ill people don't function in society".

This ill-informed response, from a professional, exposes society's misunderstanding that if you appear to be functioning, if you are showing up to work, making your appointments, honouring your commitments, and visibly keeping things together, you can't possibly be suffering with a mental illness.

In addition, following a diagnosis of a mental illness, you suddenly lurch to the other extreme. You are written off, labelled as failure, dismissed as a burden, and viewed as being unable to function in society.

But mental health is not black and white, mental health is a spectrum of infinite shades of grey. Not a linear spectrum but, like other injuries and illnesses, a multi-dimensional continuum of grey.

One axis is visible symptoms, another axis is invisible symptoms. The spectrum is further complicated as it is unique to each individual depending on their situation, history, recovery, severity, and mental/physical fitness.

If you break a leg, it not only has a visible impact but also causes psychological damage which is exacerbated by the type of break, how it affects your mobility, your life, and the recovery period.

If you suffer from a mental illness, the invisible consequences take over your life but, to a trained, experienced eye, the visible challenges are also very evident.

No-one, especially those that appear in control of their lives, is exempt from the devastating effects of poor mental health and the response to their brave admission has a dramatic impact.

"So, when a "high functioning" person asks for help or admits to himself and to someone else his struggles, it takes a lot of bravery. These people have worked every single day to build a "normal" world for themselves, they are terrified of admitting mental illness, and when they finally do and are met with rejection, little understanding, and no empathy from a mental health worker, it is devastating."

Terrified to admit mental illness or unaware of the cause of their struggles allows the shades of grey to darken quickly. Earlier recognition, greater understanding, and better support can restrict the progress through the spectrum to the lighter greys and allow a quicker return to brighter times.

And, as I've been finding out recently, it's easier to catch up when you aren't left floundering in dark, paralysing treacle!

Be aware.

Knockbacks

27th January 2019

One of the hardest, frustrating, and demoralising stages of a battle with a mental illness is when you start to feel more yourself but circumstances, situations, memories, or other people's misunderstanding knocks you back.

As you have started to feel better, the knockback feels worse than previous declines, the prospect of recovery is severely dented and your outlook for the future becomes bleak.

This is your mental illness trying to regain the control that you have successfully wrestled from its grasp.

You've already shown your strength, you've reached heights that you never envisaged reaching before you started your recovery and you've rediscovered your worth, even if others refuse and fail to recognise it.

One of the biggest moments in my battle was when I recognised that situations kept trying to knock my back. But my reaction to those situations helped me realise that I'd already taken positive steps and the strength I'd gained helped me take the small steps to keep and increase control, whatever was thrown in my path.

Positive steps forward build resilience against negative setbacks.

Keep stepping, you are worth it!

Being a bit Bolshie

31ˢᵗ January 2019

I had a short but enlightening chat at Church last Sunday with a lady who has had her fair share of medical problems over the last few years.

We both agreed that when dealing with health issues, a certain degree of stubbornness was really important. She used the term "being a bit bolshie!"

And then she went on to say that as well as challenging and fighting the illness, you also need to use common sense to avoid unexpected setbacks from over committing or over stretching during your recovery.

Using common sense is very difficult when you don't want to stop challenging your illness or when you are starting to feel better. But if you are too bolshie and don't use any common sense, you stand the chance of failing in your recovery and damaging the confidence you have built.

On the other hand, too much common sense and not enough stubbornness can hamper your progress and leave you feeling more demoralised.

It's a fine line and a balancing act but with careful planning, consideration, and sensible bravery, slow and steady progress can be made, your confidence can be rebuilt, and the bolshiness teamed with common sense will pay off!

"The real beauty of genuine, powerful platonic love is that it can be expressed at any time, any place and anywhere!"

"True friendships never die, they may go quiet, they may become distant, they may hang by a thread, but they never die."

February 2019

Something about Trees

2nd February 2019

There's something about trees.

They bring warm shelter and cool shade.

They can instil fear or counsel the anxious.

They bend in the wind, showing strength and stability.

They feed the hungry, home the homeless, nurture nature, and clear the air.

There's something about trees!

The Red Zone

7th February 2019

A contributor to the football website, *The Anfield Wrap*, uses a term "The Red Zone" for teams that have to play at maximum capacity, just to stay in the game.

While they are in the Red Zone, they over stretch, over commit, lose their control, rush their passes, make mistakes, and are playing on the edge of capitulation.

The Red Zone can also be applied to people struggling with a mental illness when everything becomes a challenge, control is lost, mistakes made, and the fear of escalation looms large.

I've mentioned before about mental illness being a multi-dimensional spectrum of grey that is unique to each individual, the Red Zone introduces a whole new gamut to the continuum of colours.

In computing, there is a colour scheme called RGB, Red Green Blue. In the scheme, there are 255 settings of Red, 255 settings of Green, and 255 settings of blue. When those primary colours are mixed together it's possible to create 16,777,216 shades of colour.

If we ignore the blue element, when you are in your red zone, the red element is turned up to full and the green element near zero, giving a deep red colour.

Depending on your circumstances, you may not be able to reduce the setting of the red element but, through mindfulness, exercise, dietary changes, fresh air, seeing the positives, and friendly support, the setting of the green element will increase.

As the green element increases, even if the red element stays at its maximum setting, the deep red slowly changes to a shade of orange. As this reduces the burden of the red zone, and while you continue to concentrate on the green that you can change, the red setting starts to reduce, changing into a shade of yellow before finally, the first green shoots of recovery start to appear.

The red element may still influence your life but now that you have removed the pressure of the red zone and you can start to make more progress.

Sometimes it's difficult to see past the red that engulfs your life, a red that always has a presence but by changing the element that you can change, things can start to look a lot greener.

Help bring some green to someone else's life!

No Stopping Myself

9th February 2019

Because of the high winds, the bacon butty van wasn't open today so me and Coco took a different route back to the beach and we stumbled across a familiar sand dune. The sand dune that I hadn't walked up since I took my first step towards my goal and started to challenge the anxiety and fear that had riddled my mind, heart, and body for so long.

Considering the thousands of metres I've walked and climbed since that first step in October 2017, that ten-metre-high pile of sand still holds massive significance in my journey.

It's still the same height. Its loose sand still provides the same resistance. It's still a physical challenge but there was one major difference in today's ascent. Compared with just over sixteen months ago, the grip my fear had over me had long since been released and there was no stopping me!

The Power of Vulnerability

12th February 2019

In a world that views vulnerability as being weak, I recently watched a Ted Talk that seeks to show the power of vulnerability and demonstrates that vulnerability is actually the birthplace of innovation, creativity, and change.

When I was diagnosed with my mental illness, if the doctor had not seen the psychological vulnerability, that even I wasn't aware of, and concentrated on improving my visual physical health, the course of my journey would not have changed. I would have continued to languish in the dark, damaging world of anxiety-driven palpitations.

The diagnosis came as a massive shock to me as, up until that point, I either hadn't realised that I was feeling vulnerable or didn't want to admit to my vulnerability for fear of being portrayed as weak. This highlighted that, because of all the other symptoms, I wasn't capable, at the time, of seeing the true damage that had been caused and I wasn't in a fit state of mind to make rational decisions that could have had an impact on my life.

Up until that point, I'd chosen to numb the vulnerability, but we cannot selectively numb emotion.

We can't say, here's the bad stuff, here's vulnerability, here's grief, here's shame, here's fear, here's disappointment – I don't want to feel these.

You can't numb those hard feelings without numbing the other aspects or emotions, you cannot selectively numb.

So, when we numb those, we also numb joy, we numb gratitude, we numb happiness and then we are miserable, and we are looking for purpose and meaning and then we feel more vulnerable and it becomes this dangerous cycle.

By exposing my vulnerability, the doctor allowed me to start to take control and start to make steps on the road to recovery.

To let myself be seen, deeply seen, vulnerably seen.

To learn to love again with my own heart even though there was no guarantee.

To rediscover gratitude and joy, and instead of catastrophising everything to say I'm just grateful because for feeling this vulnerable means I'm alive.

And most importantly, to believe that despite all my vulnerability, I was enough.

Embracing your vulnerability is not weak, it takes courage, strength and can change everything.

Armoured Protection

16th February 2019

Vulnerability is seen as a dark emotion in today's world. An emotion that should not be portrayed let alone embraced.

At some point in our lives, possibly every minute of every day, we all feel vulnerable.

To prevent negative reaction to our vulnerability, each morning, we protect ourselves with armour.

This armour not only hides our vulnerability but is also meant to make us feel stronger and more in control.

In fact, the armour only serves to keep the vulnerability inside, weighing us down and, because of the unhappiness it brings, it makes us heavy hearted, slowly and methodically eating away at our psyche.

To deal with the grief, the pain, and the despair, we numb the vulnerability but, as vulnerability is the centre of our emotions, that also means that we can't feel love, we can't feel joy, and we can't feel empathy.

Basic human connections that we all crave but instead of living those emotions wholeheartedly, we live our lives hardheartedly. Protected but empty, alone, and even more vulnerable.

The armour brings safety and security but because we are unable to let down our guard and soften a hardened persona, the armour is the only thing that is keeping us standing, literally.

It might take a professional eye or a friend who has successfully embraced vulnerability to see past the armour and make you aware of your helplessness.

At that moment, you have a choice, to continue to hide and numb your susceptibility or have the courage to be imperfect, to recognise and embrace your vulnerability, exposing it to the harsh, cold, and unsympathetic outside world.

When I went to see the company doctor, I was wearing a full suit of armour, from head to toe. Concerned about his bias towards work, and even though physically I was feeling more settled, the only chink in my armour was around my eyes. Even though I didn't want to show it, and didn't have a name for it, I was feeling very vulnerable.

Thankfully, the doctor saw everything through that tiny gap, recognised the deep-rooted anxiety that my eyes couldn't hide, and he highlighted his concerns about my psychological vulnerability.

Ironically, given the precautions I'd taken to conceal it, my shock and disbelief was palpable.

Three months later, my counsellor seized the opportunity provided by the positive cardiology report and advised me to accept the vulnerability that had already been recognised, to challenge it, to face it, to embrace it, and use its power as a driving force in my recovery.

When I was faced with this ultimatum, my hands were tied and the decision pre-determined.

Either I continued to hide my vulnerability, all its darkness and suffer from escalating symptoms or follow the medical advice, remove my armour, become unstable, expose my vulnerability, change my path and reconnect to love, joy, and empathy.

It was that moment that changed my destiny.

Every step I took, every peak I reached, every obstacle I overcame, every battle I won, every setback I endured, and every inch of progress was fuelled by the very thing that had held me back for so long.

And because I had embraced my vulnerability, I was able to recognise and emphasise with others, to relate to their vulnerability and to let my vulnerable self be seen.

The release allowed me to start to love wholeheartedly without strings, certainty, or guarantee in a way I've never loved before, to feel deep joy, a lightness, and infinite gratitude.

The choice to expose your vulnerability to world that has other priorities is not an easy one to make. There is danger that others will misinterpret your bravery and strength for the exact opposites. Others may become upset and concerned by the previously hidden challenges that you reveal.

Take it from someone who has successfully hidden my vulnerability from even the closest members of my family for 47 of my 53 years, the definite positives far outweigh the perceived negatives.

Expose your vulnerabilities, be heard, seek the help that is available, make changes to your life (either psychologically, physically, or environmentally) to alleviate and challenge your difficulties. Peel away the armour and feel your body breathe and live again, wholeheartedly!

In Your Hands

18th February 2019

We can't decide what life throws at us, but we can decide –

which ones we catch

which ones we drop

which ones we let go over our heads and

which ones we throw straight back … and how hard we throw them!

It's in your hands!

Silence is Golden

24th February 2019

A couple of things I've noticed in the last couple of days.

Firstly, I've regained my perspective that had been so damaged by the irrational thoughts instigated by my anxiety and, secondly, I'm not as fidgety as I used to be.

Loads of things went wrong with the audio/visual stuff at Church this morning. Things that in the grand scheme of things are soon forgotten. As I stood on the balcony trying to balance the microphones, a smile came across my face as I realised that in the past those things would have caused all sorts of irrational reactions to fill my already overflowing brain, raised my anxiety, and maybe caused a bout of palpitations. But today, and over the last few weeks, I took my calmness as another sign that my perspective is being restored.

Last night, I went out for a lovely meal with Kay and friends and during the meal it was noticed that I wasn't tapping my fingers and my feet and fidgeting as much as I usually do.

I said that, for the first time in ages, I didn't have any music going through my head, so I didn't have anything to tap along to, and maybe the lack of music was because I felt more relaxed, less anxious, and less nervous. Maybe the music was to mask my heartbeat or cover over my anxious thoughts.

Whatever the explanation, the silence is golden!

Bloom Again

26th February 2019

Once you realise that you are in a battle with your mental health, YOU have a choice.

Do you continue to fight with the dirt that life and others cover you with, to fuel the negativity with your comments and allow the challenges to continue to drag you deeper into the darkness?

Or

Do you change direction, do you use the challenges presented by the dirt as nutrients, to strength your will, to reframe the obstacles to your advantage and help yourself grow and bloom and push towards the powerful, enriching and positive light?

It's an easy choice but a difficult problem and, I'm sorry to say, it can't simply be solved by posting inspirational quotes or memes, that may even inflame your situation and further darken your path, you have to push away from what is holding you back.

You have the will, you have the power, and, like the Lotus flower, you can bloom again, in whatever form that may take!

"Love reciprocated is love accepted!"

"Love that is unprompted and unexpected is love that is undeniable and unquestionable!"

March 2019

Life Changes

10th March 2019

I've been listening to a few podcasts led by Dr Rangan Chatterjee, including one with Dr Danny Penman, that changed my view on mindfulness.

Before listening to the podcast, my only exposure to mindfulness was a very basic breathing technique that I'd used to control my reaction to palpitations. However, as I used the technique, I thought that I was only touching the edges of mindfulness and to fully feel the benefits of this life-changing quality, I would need to learn how to meditate properly.

It was incredible to hear an expert on mindfulness talk about using the same technique to control his pain following a paragliding accident. Dr Penman then explained how this mindfulness technique can be used at any time, in any place, and for many situations.

Last weekend, for whatever reason, my heart was beating stronger and the beats felt sharper. When this happens, the ectopic beats, that when my heart is quiet can't be felt, were really noticeable and this started to raise my anxiety levels and the ectopics got a little bit worse.

After doing a walk last Saturday, when the raised anxiety levels caused me a couple of problems, and following the advice in the podcast, I used the technique with renewed confidence. The anxiety was quelled, the ectopics became less noticeable, and my confidence recovered. Since then, my heart has been blissfully quiet, and I've been noticing that my mind has been practicing the technique on lots of occasions this week. Not for any reason, just to perfect the technique even more, together with the breaking of habits that Dr Penman also recommended.

And then I listened to an incredible talk with Dr Gabor Maté and his views on addiction and how your childhood shapes your adult health.

In the podcast Dr Maté reframes commonly used words to bring a different perspective to their meanings.

He explains the difference between lifestyle changes and life changes, here's my interpretation of what he said –

"Lifestyle changes tinker round your external edges, while life changes trigger internal transformation."

I Know It Was You

13th March 2019

Today is my Nan's birthday and as my thoughts wander through the memories of our time together, my mind naturally fills with my other relatives, past and present, who have a massively inspirational impact on my life.

Their strength, perseverance, loyalty, dedication, and motivation in the face of all their challenges.

Their self-deprecating humour, effortless charm, brutal life-changing honesty, and endless love.

Their songs, strange ways, inventive games, tangent filled conversations, funny impressions, driving skills, children leading, giving more than taking, and accordion playing!

I miss all the ones that have passed but, in a strange way, I can see them whenever I want now.

I know that without them I wouldn't be here, both biologically in 1965 and in more recent times when I've often looked up to the skies, smiled, and said; "I know that was you and you and you and you and you!"

Fresh Start

17th March 2019

Eighteen years since it was last decorated and three months after I randomly decided to dismantle the wardrobes and make a start, after reading *The Subtle Art of not giving a F*, it's lovely to have a fresh, feathery, and calming mauve bedroom instead of the dated, plain, and harsh bright orange that it was before.

It's also been a big test for me.

In the past, an eight-mile dog walk on a Saturday morning would have scuppered most of the day, as my heart tried to decide how to react to the exercise.

The decorating may not be anything out of the ordinary and no mountain challenge but it's another step in my quest to regain control of my mind and body and a subtle way of showing the important things to give a F about!

Countering Doubts

21st March 2019

The first walk is always the hardest, in fact, the first incline is always the hardest.

Before then, the part of your brain reprogrammed by anxiety tries to sow seeds of doubt, muddy the waters, and trigger flare-ups.

"What if my heart's condition has deteriorated since my last check up eighteen months ago?"

"How will my recovery be?"

"Will I be breathless?"

You counter the doubts with the techniques that have helped you push the anxiety back. You step on, relax, breath, and recover.

And then it clicks and the anxiety ducks back into the black hole that it once dragged you into, the lid slams shut, and you cover it with a boulder made of confidence.

Today was my acclimatisation day in Staveley, a chance to get my mind and body back in tune with the inclines.

Eleven miles later and job done.

And then a mile from home, things went a little weird.

As we approached a gate, a lady with two dogs was in front of me and she noticed Coco's muzzle. We chatted and then walked up the road together.

The conversation naturally drifted from Coco and her dogs, Ghyll Bank (where I'm staying), Elf Howe (a house nearby where she lives), her husband's large bowels, my Heartbeat challenge, my hole in the heart, her understanding of Atrial Septum Defects and Wolff-Parkinson-White syndrome from her time as a nurse/midwife, my ablation, her son's multiple ablations, my mental illness, her husband's walking habits, CBT Counselling, breathing techniques ("breathe in when you go into cold water") and my completion of the Kentmere Round!

And all in the space of a mile!

A very uplifting walk!

Feeling Different

26th March 2019

Before I came to Staveley this year, I knew it was going to feel different to the visits over the previous seven years.

While I was struggling with my undiagnosed mental illness, the time in Staveley was an escape from the stress and anxiety that had engulfed my mind and heart. I'd try and cram as much as possible into the weekend and ended up constantly being tense and on edge as my heart would react after exercise.

Last year, my heart was more settled, but the snow brought different challenges and I was preoccupied with making unexpected progress toward the goal agreed with my counsellor and this brought extra pressure to my week.

This year, having reached the goal and completed my Heartbeat challenge and with the snow staying away, I could relax and use the confidence gained in 2018 to rebuild my fitness that had reduced over the winter, while also enjoying some quality time with family and great friends.

Yesterday was a revelation. After gradually increasing my levels of exercise last week and resting over the weekend, I did a nine-mile walk with Coco with an ascent of over 2,000 feet.

In previous years, the rest of my day would have been scuppered by battles to regulate my heartbeat. After a brief rest at the cottage, I left Coco on the couch and walked the four miles down to the village and back.

And today, I walked Coco down to the village and back before leaving her to sleep and heading over to Keswick to walk up Walla Crag, Bleaberry Fell and High Seat. Two more Wainwrights ticked off, with incredible views across the lake of ten others that I climbed last year, and awe-inspiring views of Derwent Water, Bassenthwaite Lake, Skiddaw, Blencathra and Helvellyn.

The perfect end to a perfect week.

Out of the Blue

30th March 2019

Post from 30th March 2018:

Lovely Good Friday walk from Downham, round Pendle Hill's Big End, over the summit and back to Downham. I think that might become a regular post-work walk … then I'll move on to Ingleborough. Loads of gorgeous lambs a-gamboling, a-frolicking, and a-posing, Heather Barclay! :-)

On this day last year, I walked up Pendle Hill and continued the steps I'd taken towards the goal agreed with my counsellor. The hill was the first hill on what would become my forty-five-peak challenge for Heartbeat.

To get to that point, I had to take things slowly, to build my fitness gradually, to expect setbacks, to use, practice, and hone the breathing and relaxation technique that I'd been given and slowly build the confidence that would steadily reduce the anxiety and fear that had gripped my heart for so long.

A year on, my goal reached, the challenge completed, and my anxiety reduced dramatically.

And then today, out of the blue, another couple of attempts by my anxiety to regain a foothold.

Once when I got up when my heart went temporarily fast while I was getting dressed and once when I climbed a sand dune at the end of my walk this morning.

Two more attempts and two more opportunities to use my mindfulness technique to quell and control the palpitations that have blighted my life for so long.

The mindfulness that brings relaxation to my body when tension was for so long the default reaction. The feeling at the top of the sand dune as I felt my heart go from an ectopic-beat-filled rhythm to sinus rhythm in one beat was incredible, a massive positive from a potentially negative situation.

Keep stepping, keep building confidence, and keep growing.

More evidence of the power of mindfulness!

"It's not about treating certain people differently, it's about treating everyone the same."

"Support the weak and vulnerable but don't forget to help refuel the strong and tenacious!"

April 2019

Like a lighter

11th April 2019

From 12 p.m. on April the 11th 2014 until 12 a.m. on April the 13th 2014 were possibly the worst thirty-six hours of my life.

Five years ago today, eight months after the dam protecting my heart burst under the pressure of built-up stress, and after a myriad of shorter, less challenging episodes, my heart went into debilitating, dangerous, and potentially deadly palpitations.

I initially thought the palpitations were due to a cut gum during a routine dental filling or because my heart had started to fail. However, now that my heart's stability has improved dramatically, and given that I haven't had any medical treatment or taken medication to aid my recovery, I now understand the true cause of the palpitations that could very easily have caused catastrophic failure.

Even given the massive amount of progress I've made, my heart still has moments when it tries to trigger palpitations.

Last week, when I was fighting a bug, it tried then.

Leading up to my trip to the dentist on Tuesday, it tried again.

My heart is probably always going to try and try and try again. But thankfully, I can now retain control and my heart recovers.

So, what's the difference between now and the events of those painfully frightening thirty-six hours?

I liken my heart to a lighter.

Between 2013 and 2017, when my heart unexpectedly sparked, the anxiety fuel that had accumulated over time ignited the spark causing a massive flare up of palpitations that further fuelled the fire.

It took someone to hear, someone to check, and someone to advise to help me disconnect the fuel supply, similar to the switch wheel on the lighter.

This reduced the likelihood of the spark igniting and bought me space to start to drain the fuel.

Gradually over time as my confidence grew, mindfulness took over, reducing dramatically the prospect of escalation.

Yes, given its electrical weirdness and under certain circumstances, my heart will spark again but, as proven the other day, during an intense scale and polish, the build-up of anxiety-laced fuel has been drained and the associated tension reduced.

The powerful effects of anxiety are misunderstood and underestimated in society, but my journey proves how the associated tension, uncertainty, and fear can instigate and inflame physical symptoms and cause secondary suffering.

Anxiety is more than just a state of mind.

Thought-Provoking

16th April 2019

I've just read a thought-provoking article about the negatives and positives of sharing your life with someone who lives with autism.

The lows and the highs.

The black and the white.

The dark and the light.

The fake and the reality.

The self-exclusion and the heartfelt natural connections.

The pain and the love.

The heartache and the joy.

Two paragraphs stood out....

"The upsides are he is completely accepting of every race, creed, colour, and sexuality. He doesn't think lateral he thinks literal and doesn't understand why anyone would discriminate against people for no good reason."

And....

"I once asked him if he was relieved that his sister doesn't have the same autism as him (she is on the spectrum though) and he replied, "That's a stupid thing to say, why would you consider your kid being any other way than the way she is?" and that is a brilliant Aspergers answer."

Education → Recognition → Understanding → Acceptance →

Love → Growth.

Life-Changing Conversation

23rd April 2019

I have just been down to Church to cut the grass and as I pulled into the front car park, a van turned up to deliver some polling booths.

As the driver was lifting them out, I picked one up to carry it and the driver said he'd use his trolley because he was wearing a heart monitor.

Turns out he is under investigation for Atrial Fibrillation. He's had his heart restarted a couple of times, on medication and might be able to have "a wire put inside his heart, or something like that".

When I told him that I'd had an ablation for my heart and told him to push to get one himself, he was made up to hear from someone who could relate to his struggles.

If I had turned up ten seconds earlier, he'd have missed me.

If I had turned up a few minutes later, he'd have been and gone.

If I'd cut the grass over the weekend, that potentially life-changing conversation may never have happened.

If I'd parked in the back car park, we'd never have met.

If he had decided not to mention about his heart monitor, I wouldn't have been able to share my experiences.

Mysterious ways!

SMA

28th April 2019

In the modern world of stats, targets, and allowances, when we are measured by averages based on generalisations, we can feel bombarded with the need to respond quicker, exercise longer and constantly strive to improve our personal best.

But what if, through disability, illness, or circumstances, that's not possible and the measurements mark you as a failure and, as your confidence is dented, you beat yourself up for being "below average" in the eyes of the world.

Looking back, when I was trying to recover from my undiagnosed mental illness, I set myself challenges and goals that, with hindsight, were unrealistic and unsustainable. And for every false dawn, of which there were many, my confidence, will to win, and hopes for the future all diminished a little more as the anxiety encouraged me to push harder and fail more.

This all changed when my counsellor encouraged a different approach and, after every little success, my mindset changed.

Recognising MY situation, and not that expected of me by the statisticians, we set realistic, maintainable, and achievable goals and agreed that, given MY circumstances, small steps would be required to reduce the likelihood of repeated failure.

We coined the phrase "keep stepping" to simplify the process. A phrase which I know has inspired others who, unbeknown to me until recently, are fighting similar battles.

On your journey, ignore the averages, expectations, and stats, they don't apply to an individual like you with your unique, personal challenges. Tailor your goals to your situation, make changes, either physical, mental, or environmental that suit your needs and not those laid down by the modern world.

Visit, enjoy, and appreciate the beauty of the natural world.

Walk at your pace, headphones off, listen to the many and varied sounds, both natural and man-made that surround you and give your brain time and space to process the thoughts that whirl through your mind.

Acknowledge them, expose them, challenge them, and rationalise them, reducing their hold, relinquishing their control and pushing back on the anxiety that relies on them.

SMA - Small (steps), Maintainable (steps), Achievable (steps)…

And if you are struggling and the fear of failure looms again, keep stepping in whatever way is manageable by you.

Take care and be your personal best.

"Make the ordinary extraordinary."

"Ignore the idiots, they've worked hard to earn that moniker, don't make it easy for them to add your name to their list!"

May 2019

Two Legends

3rd May 2019

I can't think of a better day to reach 28,000,000 steps since May 2014.

It's a massive testament to the amazing skill of Dr Hamilton and his team whose open heart surgery on the 3rd of May 1973 has not only allowed me to reach that milestone, and honour his work, but also withstand the thirty-three years of Supra Ventricular Tachycardia and four years of anxiety-driven palpitations.

And then there's Coco who has been my almost constant companion throughout those millions of steps. Cajoling, encouraging, supporting, and, most importantly, creating space and opportunity to regain control of my mental and physical fitness.

I'm not sure where I'd be without those two legends!

Keep stepping!

No Need to Fight

6th May 2019

Among all the potato peelings, pot washing, early mornings, late nights, eighteen-hour-non-stop days, sizzling sausages, arrow shooting, wall climbing, night-time duties, rounders, hundreds of questions, and endless "Mike Mike Mike"'s, a quiet voice mindfully reminded me of how things had changed from the last four visits to Kirkham.

The voice recalled the weekends full of forced chores as I fought battles with things that, at the time, I didn't understand.

I'd get up early to peel the spuds in the quickest possible time, move from task to task without a break, make the days last as long as possible and frantically clean the rooms at the end of our stay.

All in a vain hope that it would benefit my health.

With hindsight, the forcing had no positive effect, it just induced tiredness for days on end and had little impact on the underlying symptoms.

Now that I understood my predicament, the mindfulness helped me recognise that I was no longer fighting or forcing things. I'd catch myself smiling at the previously stressful situations, take time to pause, allow others to share the load, and relax whenever possible.

A busy, potentially explosive, and, at times, challenging weekend was a great success, no tiredness and another big step in the right direction.

"Mindfulness is recognising that instead of forcing and fighting things that you don't understand, you start to understand that you don't need to fight and force things anymore."

Anxiety is a Thief

11th May 2019

It's Mental Health Awareness week next week and I've thinking about anxiety on the beach this morning, just letting my unhindered mind wander …

Anxiety is a thief that skulks around in the dark and hides away in the shadows, waiting for the opportunity to break into your thoughts and ransack your mind.

It's an anti-social coward that does everything to avoid exposure, knows every trick in the book, has an answer for everything, it clouds your reality and hates being recognised.

It's misunderstood, surrounded by stigma, and encourages discrimination. It can arrive unexpectedly, have a personal invitation, or be imposed on you by others or circumstances.

It's not an illness, not a disease, not a syndrome and in many people's minds it's just a "just". It can cause physical reaction and inflame pre-existing physical conditions.

It's a difficult to dislodge squatter that not only wants to devastate your mind but can steal your –

Family
Friends
Patience
Concentration
Motivation
Dedication
Determination
Time
Career
Health
Standing
Focus
Fight
Fitness
Fortitude
Life
Confidence
Socialization
Education
Recall
Intelligence

Resolve
Will
Success
Cohesion
Speech
Coordination
Trust
Ambition
Vocalisation
Stability
Control
Desire
Libido
Direction
Vocabulary
Balance

It can be nipped in the bud with trained recognition, resolved quickly with the right support or left to fester, to burrow deeper and deeper and become ensconced.

In my experiences there are ten stages of the battle, the severity of each stage is dependent on the level of damage caused. Every stage has the potential to send you back to "Go" but once you're aware, once you are tooled up and once you are supported, the chances are reduced.

Here are the stages:

Recognition
Reaction
Recovery
Regain
Realisation
Refocus
Rebuild

Reconnection

Reinstate

Restart

Keep stepping, keep talking, keep exposing and together we'll get there!

Proving Fear Unfounded

16th May 2019

I just watched a powerful documentary by someone who on the outside appears to have everything in perfect order but on the inside, she is battling severe anxiety that dates back to traumatic events from her childhood.

Great British Bake-Off Winner Nadiya Hussain's counsellor recognised that the controls she is putting in place, in a hope to keep the anxiety at bay, is actually fuelling the fear that she has been battling for the majority of her life.

As my counsellor did with me, her counsellor took an educated gamble by telling her to push back on her anxiety, introduce randomness and impulse into her life, to prove that her fears were unfounded.

After initial progress, slight and expected setbacks brought a grinding halt to her hopes of a "cure".

Then the realisation that in this world of instant fixes, immediate responses, and instantaneous gratification, the battle for improved mental well-being is long, hard, and challenging.

That the responsibility for recovery is in the hands and mind of the person living with the anxiety.

That they can push back, they can challenge, they can expose, they can take back control and they can destroy the "monster" that has gripped their life for so long.

Well done Nadiya!

Psychological Battle
20th May 2019

Last week, as it does from time to time, my heart decided to beat mischievously.

I think the main reason was that I was involved in a number of discussions surrounding Mental Health Awareness Week and I believe that memories of my battles raised my anxiety levels sufficiently to trigger extra heart beats which threatened to start longer bouts of palpitations.

On Thursday night, as I sat watching Nadiya Hussain's documentary "Anxiety and Me" on iPlayer, my heart was throwing in an extra beat for every fourth normal beat. The extra beats are harder than the normal beats and because they happen slightly out of sync, they are very noticeable and impossible to ignore.

Watching Nadiya's demonstration of how she uses a "tried and trusted" technique to deal with an anxiety attack brought back memories of how I used to react when my heart would explode into palpitations.

As Nadiya breathed deeply in through her nose and aggressively out of her mouth, you could see the tension increase in her body until she was nearly physically sick.

During an anxiety attack, when your heart rate is already elevated, your breathing rate has increased and your blood pressure is raised, the forced introduction of additional tension, oxygen, and pressure can only overload a system that is already on the edge.

Similarly, when my heart used to beat erratically, I'd immediately become excessively tense, I'd start to fight the symptoms and try to physically force my heart to normal rhythm. That increase in tension and that forced fight only exacerbated the situation and gave my anxiety the fuel it needed to take things to another dangerous level.

Nadiya's technique is a well-known "solution" that is promoted across society as a means of reducing the effects of anxiety attacks but, in mindful reality, it only serves to compound the severity of the problem and intensify the symptoms.

It was very enlightening to see Nadiya's counsellor turn things on their head when he advised that she switched to a more mindful approach.

To accept that the panic attack was happening.

To realise that her anxiety was irrational.

That the childhood trauma that triggered the attacks was not going to happen again.

That she was safe and that she could regain control and, eventually over time, she could stop the anxiety in its tracks.

On Saturday night, I enjoyed a pint of Guinness. At the height of my challenges, I gave up alcohol as I had recognised that it would induce palpitations but recently I've been able to drink a little more without it affecting things too much.

At 4.30 a.m. on Sunday morning, I was woken up by my heart beating out of sync. One of my beats appeared intoxicated by the alcohol and was slurring its beat.

Bum bum bum blurp – bum bum bum blurp – bum bum bum blurp.

For several hours, a psychological battle raged in my mind as my anxiety seized the opportunity and tried to get me to react in the same way Nadiya had and encourage the drunken beat to infiltrate the more sober beats. Meanwhile my brain calmly advised caution and to employ the mindful technique that I had successfully used hundreds of times since September 2017.

There were moments when my heart started to race, times when multiple extra beats would fire in quick succession, times of quiet when I thought the battle was over, only for a random beat to relight the anxiety again and bring my jumbled beat back into focus.

Climbing stairs, bending over, getting dressed all served to raise my heartbeat and the associated anxiety even more but I continued, undeterred, to be present, mindful, and calm.

And then, probably as the alcohol wore off, the inebriated beat sobered up and my heart returned to a quiet, regular hum.

Once again, the power of mindfulness had conquered the weakness of my anxiety, subduing a potentially devastating situation, allowing me to enjoy a walk along the gorgeous Lune valley in peaceful serenity and it felt amazing.

Keep stepping, ready for the next battle!

Different Path

31st May 2019

Post from 31st May 2018:

Another three hills completed on The Ribena Tour; Grit Fell, Brownley Hill, and Ward's Stone! The walk was ten miles and I only met one person on my way round, a lady jogging with her dog. I stopped to have a chat with Meg the sheepdog and the lady asked where I was going and she said I was keen. I explained that I was trying to get my fitness back after my battle with anxiety. Turns out she is a part time farmer and also a Cognitive Behavioural Therapist at Lancaster and Morecambe hospitals. It was really nice to spend five minutes, in the middle of nowhere, talking about my counselling, my progress and receiving her affirmation for the steps I'd taken. A real boost and a very spooky encounter!

This time last year, I had just completed my sixth, seventh, and eighth peak over 450m and the idea of completing 45 peaks to celebrate the 45th anniversary of my heart operation was starting to take shape. I decided to keep the challenge quiet until I was sure that I could succeed.

I now see that period as a time of gaining a foothold and establishing a bridgehead in preparation for the war that I was going to have to fight against the anxiety that had terrorised my mind and body for so long.

Gradually, as I ascended the remaining 37 peaks, I won many battles; retaking ground previously lost to my enemy, rebuilding confidence damaged by previous attacks, and eventually regaining control of my mind, body, and life.

Shortly after completing my challenge, I excitedly looked forward to climbing more hills, trying to reach greater heights and conquering more Wainwrights.

Due to a variety of reasons, seven months on and apart from two peaks reached in March, I haven't really progressed past the goal reached last October.

For a few months, the lack of progress has been a source of frustration as I've searched for the next sign of progress and the need for a new goal.

Then last week, a Facebook post by Dr Gabor Maté reminded me of a podcast I'd heard earlier in the year and his book that I'd started to read called "When the Body Says No: The Cost of Hidden Stress".

I then found a vast array of videos from Dr Maté on YouTube and selected one at random.

Dr Maté is a well-renowned Physician who, unlike many other Physicians, has irrefutable proof that mental and physical health are inextricably linked. He believes that childhood trauma, suppressed poorly managed anger and emotions, chronic long-term stress, and poor self-care lead to a suppressed immune system and chronic illnesses, such as cancer, multiple sclerosis, Crohn's disease and heart disease etc.

In the video he reviews several Obituaries of people who were diagnosed with terminal illnesses. People who, even when they were receiving chemotherapy, refused to slow-down, kept pushing themselves to the limit, never stopped putting others first, and didn't seek psychological assistance.

He also refers to another patient, an executive at Microsoft, who after being diagnosed with cancer was given one year to live. She resigned from her job, rested while she received treatment, reconnected with her authentic self, became spiritually aware of psychological challenges, and recently celebrated ten years since her diagnosis.

It was then that I realised that I'd inadvertently chosen a different path. That I had no need to keep pushing myself and putting myself in danger.

Now that the war had been won, I could lay down my arms and start to win over hearts and minds, improve my knowledge of mindfulness and look to increase the awareness in society of the damage that mental illness can initiate.

I'd recognised that my anxiety had also taken a different approach, relying on guerrilla tactics of random attacks to try and re-establish itself but as Dr Maté ended his video with this sentence –

"The biggest stress of all is trying to be who you are not, the maintenance of health mainly depends on knowing who you are, getting in touch with your body, getting in touch with yourself, being mindful of all that and honouring who you are."

I realised that my next goal was to continue to find myself, to realise that I no longer had to fight, to recognise my authenticity, and to continue to educate others.

"Don't dwell on the destructive negatives, accentuate the enriching positives.

For although negativity spreads faster than positivity, good things come to those who wait!"

"We all have threads running through our lives, weave the bad ones into a strong web to catch you when you fall, and use the good ones to pull yourself back up again!"

June 2019

The Little Blighter

4th June 2019

Post from 4th June 2014:

Went to see Dr Fox today - the cardiologist, not the cheesy DJ - and although he wasn't very impressed with the workmanship of my 1970's scar he did think my ECG was weird but perfectly normal given the type of surgery I had way back when....just need to catch the little blighter in the act of messing up my Bundle of His now!

Five years after this cardio check-up and it turns out we were looking for the little blighter in the wrong place.

No amount of ECGs, Echocardiograms, twenty-four-hour heart monitors or palpitation-reducing drugs would have had any effect.

Meanwhile, undetected and unfettered, the little blighter was creating havoc in my head, mischievously altering my default reaction to everyday situations, constantly releasing stress hormones which reduced the effectiveness of my immune system and led to a psychosomatic (physical) reaction in my heart.

The destructive negative power of poor mental health in action.

And then the tables were turned, the little blighter exposed, the little blighter challenged, the little blighter defeated and gradually, patiently and mindfully a calmer default reaction, so alien in today's society, has returned, my Vagus Nerve is conveying more positive messages from my brain to my vital organs and there's more peace in my heart.

The enriching, positive, life-enhancing, uplifting, strengthening power of improved mental well-being.

Truly Uplifting

13ᵗʰ June 2019

If you are suffering from anxiety, disabled by fear or struggling with tiredness etc., I recommend you connect with Sally Bee on Facebook.

Sally is an inspiration to many of her followers. She has suffered five heart attacks in the last 15 years, three in 2004 and two a few years ago. She suffers from SCAD (spontaneous coronary artery dissection) and was not expected to live through the day when she had her first three heart attacks.

In her posts there are a lot of references to heart recovery but also more general advice for people suffering from anxiety etc., e.g. –

Listening to your body and acting on what it is telling you.

 Resting when your body is tired

Combating fear through positive thinking

Recognising that your mind can't hold two thoughts at the same time, replace the negative thoughts with positive ones

Seeking help from fellow sufferers

Seeking medical help when necessary

Exercising as you are able

Checking your diet

Living life to the full, each and every day.

Given what Sally has been through, she puts a lot of other people's "problems" in perspective and her views on life are truly uplifting.

Making a Difference

18th June 2019

As you know, I've used mindfulness extensively during my recovery and I've benefited tremendously from the technique's ability to bring breathing space to an anxious, overloaded mind and calm to an erratic, out of control heart.

The warm sense of calm that mindfulness brings to my whole psyche feels amazing as it tends to any brief negative thoughts, soothes my nervous system, reduces overactive hormone releases, and smooths the interconnections to my internal organs. But that feeling of calm has the effect of increasing my reluctance to step out of my newly found comfort zone and could potentially reduce my drive to challenge the root causes of my mental illness.

And with a $4 billion mindfulness industry reliant on selling the "product" that brings personal calm in today's stressful world, the last thing the corporately backed mindfulness "advocates" want is for the very things that push people to scramble for mindful help to change.

More stress = more mindfulness = more money, capitalism at its finest.

But there is another way.

One of the other by-products of mindfulness is that it can bring greater awareness to the struggles of others and of the wider world and, when we are ready, an increased motivation to help others in similar situations and make changes to our local environment, without feeling overwhelmed by the sheer enormity of the problems faced by so many over such a wide area.

We may not be able to change the inner workings of large corporations, e.g. Google or Facebook, but by raising issues, encouraging conversations, highlighting necessary change, and supporting others, we can help change the culture in our places of work.

Similarly, we can't clean up all the litter, but we can remove a bag's worth of rubbish from our local beach or field and encourage others to do the same.

Without the power of mindfulness, I would still be working from home on a regular basis (to prevent escalation of my heart problems) and I'd be unable to support the current drive to change an ingrained culture. Without a stable heart, my weekly walks down the beach would be impossible and the litter would return to the sea on the next tide.

Individually, we can't change the world, but we can make a difference and the more mindful we are about our thoughts, our reactions, our physicality, and, by going against the wishes of the capitalists, our local community we can make differences to things within our reach.

Keep making a difference!

Recovery is Not Linear

11th June 2019

At the end of March 2019, a close friend and colleague sadly and unexpectedly passed away. I'd known and worked with Harold since 1987 and his personality shone through in everything he did. His joy of life, cheery outlook, and infectious sense of humour endeared him to everyone he met. His passing was felt by everyone who knew him, and he will be greatly missed.

One of Harold's favourite pastimes was walking in the Lake District and he especially enjoyed camping in his caravan near Derwent Water. To celebrate his life, two walks were organised around Derwent Water for his family, friends, and colleagues to raise money for Keswick Mountain Rescue.

Although the two walks for Harold were very similar, both around the same lake even if they were in different directions, they couldn't have been more contrasting for me.

No one else on the walks would have noticed the disparity between the two walks, to them it was all internal, hidden, and invisible.

Just before the first walk, I became anxious. I wanted the walk to be a success for Harold's family, for everyone to meet up on time, for the weather to stay fine and for it to be a fitting tribute to a wonderful man, nothing too much and nothing too little.

As I walked the mile from the car park, the anxiety triggered extra beats that although didn't develop into anything that prevented me from completing the walk, brought my attention back to my heart and I started to monitor its beat constantly.

Soon after the walk started, when my anxious concerns had been addressed, my heart returned to its normal beat but throughout the walk my legs felt heavy and my stride ponderous, the effects of the earlier challenges continued to weigh heavily on my mind.

Yesterday was completely different.

I still had anxious thoughts, faced possibly challenging situations, and wanted the walk to be another success but, despite all this, as I left my car, I was completely relaxed, no palpitations, no monitoring, no heavy legs.

I took the bull by the horns, faced the situations that could have been challenging and did what I needed to do, on my terms, under my control. This time the walk was a breeze, not a struggle, and unlike on the first walk, the physical and psychologically dark threatening cloud that hung over my head was replaced by dazzling, powerful, warming light.

The first walk proved again that my anxiety, even though it has been pushed back into the shadows, still has the potential to knock me off my stride but following that walk I managed to mindfully reconcile the reasons behind its attempted resurgence. Its hope was to make me wobble and lose sight of my goal but by standing firm, my mindfulness-empowered confidence actually took me a step closer to my objectives.

Recovery is not linear, the path is not straight, obstacles will try to hinder your progress, darkness may engulf your mind, but you need to keep stepping mindfully into the light!

A Glimmer of Hope

25th June 2019

Post from 25th June 2018:

The further I walk, the higher I climb, the quicker I recover, the more I discover.... What an ignorant, insensitive, indiscriminate, intolerable, destructive, demeaning, deadly, demonic, frustrating, frightening, fractious, frantic, time-wasting, life-changing, brain-damaging, soul-destroying little shit that anxiety is and don't let anyone tell you different.... The further I walk, the higher I climb. The quicker I recover, the more I discover that it can be defeated! :-) #mentalhealthawareness #notjustanxiety

Ironically, when I wrote this post last year it was three years to the day since my anxiety had taken me to my lowest point.

June 25th 2015, nearly two years after my anxiety-riddled heart had started to fail and nearly two years until my diagnosis.

At that time, my anxiety had full control of my mind, creating havoc in my body, and it knew that it didn't have to work very hard to push me further and further down.

Innocent, innocuous, indirect comments made during meetings, increased pressure to make decisions at the Church garden party and seeing others being supported while I was left to silently flounder.

All minor but given the state of my mind and my body at time, all potentially deadly.

And then a glimmer of hope.

The other day I found the email that I sent to Kay as I walked along the coastal road on this day in 2015. I had to get out to try and make sense of my scrambled mind. To try and see a future of peace. To try and find my voice that had been silenced.

The email says it all. The confused ramblings, the irrational overreactions to minor inconveniences, the desperate plea for help and without a voice, the only way I could try to explain.

Was that email a turning point? Maybe. It gave me a glimpse of the reason behind my challenges, it allowed me to recognise that I'd lost the last five summers and it gave me a chance to reach out to outside world.

Up until that point the master of the dark arts had forced me to keep everything within so even my nearest and dearest weren't aware but now they were, and I could start to level out.

As it says in this post from last year, anxiety is still a little shit, but it can be recognised, it can be challenged, it can be exposed, it can be controlled, and it can be defeated.

"Firmness is the decisive person's implementation of strength."

"Having inner strength is a blessing until people assume that because you are strong there can't be anything wrong!"

July 2019

When the Body Says No

2nd July 2019

I've just finished reading a book called "When the Body Says No: The Cost of Hidden Stress" by Dr Gabor Maté, a renowned Canadian Physician.

The book is both challenging and enlightening as Dr Maté outlines his thoughts of the links between childhood trauma, excessive levels of stress, poorly managed anger, lack of self-care, and the onset of life-changing adult illnesses. It's both interesting and scary as he explains the effect that not only your own childhood, but your parents' and grandparents' lives, have on your possible future and how you react to certain situations, i.e. your default reaction.

My childhood, and the lives of my parents and grandparents, set me up for an incredible adulthood but despite the support I received in my early years, my default reaction was distorted by the trauma I experienced surrounding my life-long heart problems.

I don't remember my first seven years, but given the later diagnosis of Wolff-Parkinson-White syndrome and the lengthy attacks of palpitations I experienced after my open-heart surgery at the age of seven, I assume that those formative years were a struggle as my heart most likely exploded in to disabling palpitations.

Years seven to twenty-one were very similar, but I remember vividly having to sit and wait for my heart to self-revert from 200+ bpm to 70 bpm and the numerous visits to hospital. But I think my default reaction was influenced to the greatest extent from the ages of twenty-one to thirty-eight.

After being transferred to the outpatient care of an adult hospital, my new cardiologist showed me a technique that I could use to revert my heart after exercising. The technique changed my life but, as it was very brutal in its approach, also changed my default reaction from patiently waiting to forcefully controlling my heart.

When the palpitations were stopped in 2004, via a catheter ablation, I hoped my heart challenges were over, but in 2013, when a new form of palpitation started, I was faced with a dilemma.

My default reaction told me to brutally force the palpitations to stop but, as they were different, I didn't feel confident enough to use that default technique. This led to tension and my body being constantly in fight or flight mode with the associated hormones being released relentlessly and the knock-on effect that had on my whole psyche.

Thankfully counselling came to my rescue and, after experiencing and developing a greater understanding of mindfulness, slowly my default reaction changed to a more peaceful, gentle and sensitive response and the undoubted benefits that brought to my life.

As well as reducing the occurrences of palpitations, and increasing the control of any that started, my default reaction to other situations in life has also changed. I've always been laid back but without any real appreciation of the problems that can bring. Taking on too much, hiding health concerns, and poorly managed anger.

And that's where the book comes in.

Dr Maté explains the importance of looking after yourself, becoming more proficient at saying "no", being a bit more selfish, expressing anger in the right, more beneficial way, and altering the default reaction formed by your childhood and, possibly, by your ancestors.

At the end of the book, he talks about the power of negative (yes negative) thoughts and he questions the damage caused by false positivity which pushes people on with little regard to the negative implications, e.g. training to run a marathon while dealing with chemotherapy instead of allowing your body to rest and recover.

He outlines his approach to a more genuine positivity which doesn't mask the negative situations that life in general, and in particular a life blighted by illness, throws in our path.

One sentence stands out when dealing with requests for our time and talents that may lead to a greater burden on our lives and bodies –

"If a refusal (to take on extra responsibility) saddles you with guilt, while consent leaves resentment in its wake, opt for the guilt. Resentment is soul suicide."

In this quote, Dr Maté is not suggesting we become totally selfish but through the use of his "Seven As" we become more aware of the effects of not being able to say "no" and being taken for granted. To push back, for our own sake.

The Seven As? Acceptance. Awareness. Anger. Autonomy. Attachment. Assertion. Affirmation.

As I said, given its subject matter, it was a difficult book to read. It's definitely not a trendy self-help book with fancy memes and soundbites but, given his unorthodox approach, it is well worth persevering with right to the end.

It has certainly given me a greater insight into my journey and a different view on my future approach to potentially harmful situations.

Checking My Demons

4th July 2019

I've been meaning to resurrect my Thursday evening hikes for a few weeks but kept forgetting to take my boots to work.

Given the significance of today, two years after my diagnosis of mental illness, there was extra incentive to remember my boots and there was only one place to take them.

The place that once my demons ruled the paths and slopes, a place where last July I pushed back and a place where last October they were exorcised, with the help of three friends.

The plan for tonight was not to climb a number of peaks, unlike this time last year, numbers are no longer important, tonight was all about checking.

Checking if the demons had reincarnated.

Checking if the demons had regrouped.

Checking if the demons had regained a foothold.

Checking that I still ruled those paths and slopes.

They hadn't, I did!

I only wanted to reach the first peak out of the ten we conquered last October and as I climbed that first hill, it became abundantly clear the extent of the miracle that was performed on that day in 2018, especially given the context of my mind and body at the time and, without the support of those three friends, how close I came to failure.

Thinking Negatively

7th July 2019

Since reading the penultimate chapter of Dr Gabor Maté's book, I've been thinking negatively, yes negatively!

Yet in a world, especially one that surrounds a recovery from mental illness, where total positivity is seen as the only way to bring light to a dark world, Chapter 18 – "The Power of Negative Thinking" – is an enlightening beacon that even outshines all the positive brightness.

While the title of the chapter may have taken me by surprise, the content made perfect, refreshing, and logical sense.

Then I remembered I'd heard it all before.

At my second CBT Counselling session, my counsellor outlined three points that he knew would give me the best chance of recovery.

1. Challenge your anxiety

2. See the reality

3. Expect setbacks.

Although, initially, the first two points filled me with dread, that feeling quickly turned to positivity as my first steps brought dramatic progress. However, I continued to struggle with the third point.

Surely negativity was not in the counsellor's job description.

Why didn't he follow the lead of the majority of the mental health self-help groups that had swamped the Internet and YouTube?

Why didn't he tell me to leave his office and go and buy seven pairs of brightly coloured floral pants with a smiley face on and write "Be Positive" on them?

Looking back, that third point was the most important of the three.

My counsellor knew that point one would trigger point three and point two would only be satisfied when I acknowledged and accepted point three.

He knew that life would throw negative moments at me and without his honesty about reality, they would piss me off, rendering any positive pants porous and no amount of therapy or mindfulness would stop the downward flow.

True to his word, there have been many setbacks. Most notably a week later when Coco was attacked by a dog, then six months after my counselling finished, I had setbacks in the snow in Staveley and just before my final step towards my goal, my heart reacted.

All negative moments that, thanks to the advanced insight from my counsellor, I expected and was able to accept and react in the most positive way, increasing my confidence and instead of being knocked back, I could continue to step on.

But there's another major benefit to this approach.

Expecting, accepting, and even embracing the fact that negative moments will occur doesn't diminish the power of positivity, in fact it expands its scope and allows greater freedom.

False, forced positivity can have a devastating negative effect on someone battling to recover from a mental illness.

Pressure from well-meaning friends encouraging you to pull up your positive pants and socialise when, because you've hit a sight setback, all you want to do is rest. Your friends, unintentionally, take this as a sign that you are relapsing and try harder, potentially making your situation worse.

But because you are aware, because you are ready, because you have accepted the setback, you can tolerate their cajoling, calmly explain your situation, take time to rest, mindfully deal with the setback and bounce back empowered, revitalised and invigorated.

You then realise that there is no longer any pressure to appear perfect, that there's no need to paint a smile on your face, no need to use Snapchat filters to improve your body image, it becomes easier to put up with negative, insensitive, and inadequate people and tolerate those that just don't "get it".

And then, with the pressure off and the expectations diminished, the negative moments reduce, and you can push on at your own pace, secure in the knowledge that any future negative moments, which will undoubtedly occur, can be seen and dealt with in a positive light.

Positive steps from life's negative situations.

Release the Weight

9th July 2019

Strength is not hiding your feelings behind a fake smile or a flimsy wall of false positivity, they just allow your unfettered weaknesses to fester and spread until your body breaks down.

It's normal to not feel good all the time.

It's ok not to feel ok.

It takes strength to show your true feelings and ask for help.

You owe it to your mind, your body and your future to release the weight.

Inherently Flawed

11th July 2019

You've got to feel sorry for a cup of coffee, a bar of chocolate, a shopping trip, and a glass of wine.

We expect them to wake us in the morning, get us through the day, provide therapy, and relax us in the evening, while not preventing us from sleeping.

A lot of pressure on their inanimate shoulders.

They do have their benefits, but when used to cover a mental illness, every gulp, every chomp, every purchase, and every sip only serve to hide the true reason behind the struggles that they are meant to address.

Fuel is added to the fire, intensifying its heat, reducing the effect of future stimulants and increasing the dose required to continue to disguise the truth.

As the internal, masked heat is inadvertently turned up, the dependency on the pick-me-ups increases proportionately, further inflaming the hidden challenges leading to escalation, perpetual reactions, increased mental and physical health concerns, and the possibility of addiction looms large.

The modern world's promotion of intoxicants to deal with psychological issues is inherently flawed, and possibly encouraged by the manufacturers to increase sales.

But there is another instinctive, complimentary, non-addictive, potent, side-effect-free way and it all lies right between our own shoulders.

Mindfulness, the ability to achieve a second of breathing space in a chaotic mind.

A second that expands into a moment, the moment into an hour, the hour into a day, the day into a week, the week into a lifetime.

A second that brings a semblance of peace, a glimpse of order, a glimmer of light, an increase in confidence.

A second that reveals a different path, a reduction in dependency, an opportunity to expose and challenge the hidden reality behind the defensive barrier built on flimsy highs.

Mindfulness, an asset to approach the barricade, to scale its ineffectual walls, to dismantle brick by brick the concealed impediment and step on to a brighter future.

Mindfulness, the power to bring focus to an anxious mind, to reinvigorate senses subdued by the brain's pre-occupation and the confidence to assertively rationalise tiring thoughts and re-establish overlooked self-care.

With your senses revived you can take time to savour the aroma of the finest arabica beans, let the deluxe cocoa melt in your mouth, calmly select your next desired acquisition free from guilt and relish the taste of the hand-picked grapes in a mature fine wine.

With the pressure reduced, the mind and body start to synchronise, sleep hygiene improves, cravings subside, awareness is raised, and future recurrences, hopefully, prevented.

One Small Step

20th July 2019

Living with a physical or mental illness puts your life in the Red Zone, where your body is working harder just to stay in the game, everything becomes a challenge and the slightest setback threatens to tip you over the edge.

With a physical illness or injury, we are limited in the steps we can take to reduce the intensity of the Red Zone and, like in the case of my two physical conditions, we need to rely on the talents of skilled doctors and surgeons to hopefully provide relief from the pain and the suffering.

With a mental illness the focus turns to you and, although it's probably the last thing you feel like doing, the onus is on you to take responsibility for reducing the severity of your symptoms.

In my second hour of counselling, when I was advised to challenge my anxiety and see the reality, it soon became clear that I'd have to fight the majority of the battle on my own.

Understandably, as I didn't have a clue what to do or how I was going to do it, I was filled with dread.

The choice was stark, either stay in that shitty place for longer or grab this chance by the balls and take steps to gradually change things.

Steps that on the surface seem too simple, like gentle exercise (Thanks Coco), to have any effect but each shoot of green that sprouted in my life slightly diluted the depth of the red making the next step slightly easier and its benefits more noticeable.

At the time, I wasn't in a stable enough position to change the reasons behind my red zone but, as the red turned into a calmer orange with the introduction of deeper greens, breathing space brought on by mindfulness began to appear.

Breathing space that not only provided leeway for coping with any predicted and unexpected setbacks but also allowed focus to shift onto finally reducing the influence of the red that I thought would never diminish.

To coin a phrase that is very prominent at the moment, on the anniversary of the Moon landings, "One small step", and you don't have to be on the moon to take it!

Choosing Your Path

22nd July 2019

Life is full of situations, events, and choices.

A lot of the time we can't control the situations that life throws at us; illness, redundancies, bereavement, lottery wins, family, success for your favourite team.

We have slightly more control over which events we watch, we attend, and that occur in our lives; concerts, shows, sporting events, friendships, marriages, and, to a certain extent, even divorces.

We have almost total control of our choices. Which team we support, our taste in music, the clothes we wear, how we react to situations and events, do we hold grudges or practice forgiveness, whether we let our past define our lives or bravely step on to the future.

We can choose what to pick up, what to lay down, how much gossip to spread, the level of truth we share, whether we compare, compete and try to keep up with others or if we feel contentment in our current situation.

We also have a choice of what to believe, whether we recognise that people may be brought into our lives for a reason. That situations and events may occur to help us grow and flourish or hold us back and keep us stuck in the mud of resentment and anger.

Choosing your path after a challenging time is very difficult and we may wait patiently for signs or external influence to guide us.

However, almost everything may already be ready, and the guiding hand that created this defining situation is waiting for you to complete your puzzle and take responsibility for placing your final piece that will show you a brighter, lighter, clearer, and more peaceful future.

You have been gifted the power of free will and you are the only person who can decide to take responsibility for your future.

Don't waste it, time is short, make the choice, choose wisely, complete your jigsaw and see the bigger picture.

Breaking Your Mould
23rd July 2019

It's times like this morning that bring so much into perspective for me.

I slept well, felt good when I got up but soon after setting off with Coco, I started to feel the all too familiar strong and random thuds from my heart. Ectopics.

The reason that brings things into perspective is because of the change in my reaction to these unwelcome visitors.

Before I became aware of the consequences, my overly tense reaction would have triggered the release of hormones that would normally only have been required in times of threat but weren't necessary then. Hormones that only served to cause an escalation of my predicament.

Some might say that becoming tense in such a situation is a natural reaction but that couldn't be further from the truth.

The more natural reaction, even though it goes against modern day natural instincts, is to react calmly, to trigger your Vagus Nerve with all its sympathetic powers and to use the calmness and breathing space it brings to recognise and rationalise the possible causes.

In this morning's case, I realised that the ectopics were most likely being triggered by the heat. Instead of chucking fuel on the fire, by releasing inflaming hormones, this realisation cooled the situation and started to reduce the frequency and intensity of the ectopics until they stopped completely.

In a world that seems to encourage tense, angry, and instant reactions, go against the grain and react differently with a calm, considered, and conscious approach. Take it from me, it changes everything and helps to prevent long-term consequences.

At the moment, I seem to be learning something new about mental health every day.

Living in a Hostile Environment

25th July 2019

I was asked the other day why I thought mental illness was more prevalent today. One reason is more awareness and better diagnosis but the other reason, I feel, is modern technology, both in the pressures brought by social media and in our reliance on our devices to plan, control, monitor, and advise us on our journeys.

Diaries and calendars have been used for centuries to bring order to our lives, but only recently have we received automated notifications of forthcoming appointments and a better plan of our days ahead.

Maps allow us to plan our route to avoid the challenges, to keep within our physical capabilities, to find places to rest and recover to fit in with the available time, whilst ensuring that we see all the stunning views, visit all the landmarks, and increase our fitness.

GPS can accurately pinpoint where we are on our journey, which way we are facing, how high or low we are, what lies ahead, how far we've come, how far we've yet to go, to see if we've veered off course, allowing us to manually reroute, and, given our pace, when we will reach our destination.

Sat Nav plots and talks us through our journeys, recognising any obstacles in front of us, automatically rerouting our path in an instant and then guiding us down diversions with minimal disruption.

But have we become over dependent on technology that has reduced our ability to deal with unexpected events, obstacles, and setbacks?

Imagine a life filled with days of unplanned challenges when every notification induces fear and every social appointment is met with dread.

That is a life lived with a mental illness, when technology, that previously assisted and enlightened, is now your nemesis. An enemy that continues to haunt and degrade your life. A hostile environment where even the slightest negative comment can tip you over the edge. A place where you try to portray a better view whilst screaming inside for someone, anyone, to recognise your hidden struggles and reach out. But your disguise is so perfect that no one will know that you need help and your journey goes deeper into despair.

No map to plan your route, no means of avoiding challenges, pushed to the limit of your physical capabilities, no chance to rest and recover, all your views are black, landmarks are blurred, and your fitness destroyed.

No GPS to pinpoint where you are, no idea which way you are facing, no indication of how high or low you are, no warning of the dangers that lie ahead or celebrations of the successes you've already achieved. No path to follow, no view of how far you've veered off track, no idea how to reroute to reach your unseen, unknown, and uncertain destination.

No Sat Nav to talk you through your journey or to reroute you around the invisible obstacles that lie ahead. You stumble, fall, and get lost down multiple blind alleys and dead ends as you desperately try to find a diversion, any diversion.

No plan, no control, no hope, no future.

Bleak

Black

Blind

Broken

Then a friend, an ear, a hand, a chance.

They pick you up, place you back on your path, guide you past the obstacles, lift you, point you in the correct direction, clear your view, encourage you to rest and recover, to see the reality, to challenge your challenges, to see the light, to regain your footing, to start to climb, to raise your head, to clear your mind, to start to plan, to face your enemy.

Slowly you step on, mindful of your progress, equipped to regain your position, energised to grow, ready to progress, invigorated by the loving friendship.

Then you notice someone else veering off course, seeming off-kilter, appearing detached, alone, easily agitated and angered. Your increased awareness and understanding means you can step in and help them to re-orientate, redirect, reroute, and, with your support, recover.

Pass it on!

Reaping the Benefits
30th July 2019

An article in *Psychology Today* was posted on a Facebook page for Wolff-Parkinson-White syndrome the other day.

The article outlines a breathing method which simulates the Vagus Nerve to bring calm to a stressful situation and counteract the dangers associated with constant fight or flight reactions and the stress-related hormones they release.

The breathing technique focuses on the inhale-exhale ratio and the benefits of longer exhalation.

The article suggests a two-minute period, when you feel the stress building up, when you quietly concentrate on your breathing to inhale gently through your nose for four seconds then slowly exhale through pursed lips for eight seconds and repeat the cycle ten times.

Not only does this technique bring focus to your breathing, it also allows the chance to be mindful of any other parts of your body that may be reacting.

The technique can be used at any time but as with many things associated with mental health recoveries, this is not an instant on-off switch that will immediately have an effect but needs time and practice to reap the benefits, perseverance is key.

It's also worth noting that you shouldn't expect to be able to achieve the 4:8 ratio straight away. Start with a 2:4 ratio and slowly increase the lengths of each breath.

Make sure you inhale gently as a more aggressive inhalation could trigger a fight or flight reaction as your brain may take that as a sign of imminent danger.

Give it a try. This technique is very similar to the one I've been using since 2017 with all the benefits that has brought to my life.

Have a good day!

Being More Selfish

31st July 2019

One of the hardest things for a *selfless* person to do is to be more *selfish*. The word doesn't even exist in their vocabulary.

People who tirelessly give up their time and energy to perform unseen tasks which on the surface appear menial, but they know are vital to the enjoyment of others.

Yet, and I've only discovered this recently, one of the most beneficial steps for better physical and mental health is the bravery to take control, to selfishly listen to your body and decide to lay down some of those tasks for your own benefit.

This then allows you space to concentrate on you for a change and time and energy to explore other opportunities to enhance your well-being without the pressure, under your own steam and for your own benefit.

It is not a failure to lay down tasks that you've successfully completed for years, unnoticed, rarely appreciated, and unrewarded. You are not letting anyone down or accepting the inevitable.

You are reframing you and selflessly giving more time to those that love and value you and enjoy your company immensely.

Be more selfishly you!

"Even if it's painful, relive special memories you had with special people.

Time does not devalue them; they are eternally priceless!"

"A true friend just wants their friends to be happy, loved and safe … no matter the circumstances and distance that keeps them apart!"

August 2019

New Horizon

2nd August 2019

An article from the *Metro*, and shared by *Time to Change*, epitomises the challenges that people living with a mental illness face in today's society.

You can struggle for weeks, months, and years but because you force yourself to show up to work or socialise, you're deemed to be ok and not in need of any support.

Conversely, when your mental illness has been diagnosed and more publicly recognised, and because you've taken positive steps, a single good day leads to the opinion that you are cured and from that point on your struggles are behind you.

But mental illness is not a dose of the flu, a rash, or a niggly cough, where you rest, take a course of antibiotics or apply a cream and a few days later you feel better.

A mental illness reprograms your brain, alters your reactions, and plants explosives that are triggered by innocuous and everyday situations that can turn a good day into a horrendous one in an instant.

Triggers that are unavoidable, that occur in unrelated and overheard conversations, in support of others, in bad news, in internal battles, in rekindled memories and, believe it or not, in long overdue good news.

The triggers are everywhere, and they can quickly turn a light and optimistic vista into a dark and depressed tunnel and any hope of recovery appears to disappear.

But there is hope. Your diagnosis can change everything. It can provide support, medication, techniques, and a greater understanding of your challenges and how to manage them.

With greater awareness, through our experiences, we can spot the tripwires before they are inadvertently triggered.

With improved focus, and less preoccupation, we defuse the charged explosives before they detonate.

With increased confidence, and less anxiety, we can reduce the collateral damage.

With better communication, and less stigma, we can open conversations with fellow strugglers and spread the word.

Because I can talk about my mental illness and recovery, and on the surface everything in my garden appears rosy, many people may think that my mental illness has been cured. But in the last six days there have been multiple moments when my delicate house of cards could have come crashing down to the ground.

However, I showed up to work, I performed to my objectives, I supported others, I recognised, I reconciled, I continued to grow.

But I know that I'm only a footstep away from the next trigger ... so cautiously, and mindfully, I step on towards my new horizon!

Shifting the Focus

10th August 2019

Today in 2017 was a massively important moment on my journey.

The results from my Echocardiogram would shift the focus from the perceived physical damage to disarming the real assailant with its vast armoury of mind bullets.

A moment that would eventually expose the potential devastation of poorly managed and unrelenting stress, lack of understanding, poor self-care, total preoccupation, all-encompassing stigma and the body's inability to withstand constant fight or flight reactions present in today's world.

Thankfully, given its previous challenges, my body screamed "no" loud enough to be heard … eventually.

But how loud is your body shouting?

Is it time for you to start to strip back the complexities of life, to tear down the walls built as a facade for the outside world but that also serve to allow the hidden negatives to fester and damage you internally?

Is it time to be honest with yourself?

To be a bit more selfish?

To find moments that you lift you?

To find space in your mind to bravely reveal your past to a world that is becoming more understanding and more accepting?

To explore the simple, effective power of mindfulness, that has been clouded by modern world complexity, and allow your mind and body to whisper "yes"?

It's time … start stepping!

Being Present

12th August 2019

I've been practicing mindfulness meditation for twenty-three months and catch myself using it on many occasions during the day in loads of different situations.

While I'm cooking.

While I'm walking.

While I'm driving.

While I'm working.

When I'm frustrated.

When I feel the stress building up.

When my brain plays tricks.

When other people try to annoy me.

When worries surface.

When memories are triggered.

When my heart gets mischievous.

I'm not in a trance. I haven't been hypnotized. I'm here in the present moment, simply breathing in, simply aware, then simply breathing out, simply aware, simply grounded.

Leaving it Behind

14ᵗʰ August 2019

"I opened my eyes and it was there.

Got dressed and it was there.

Ate my breakfast and it was there.

Walked the dog and it was there.

Drove to work and it was there.

Sat at my desk and it was there.

It was the uninvited attendee at the meetings.

It was the pressure on my shoulders.

It was the stress in my body.

It was the anxiety in my mind.

It was the uncertainty in my heart.

It was the mask covering my face.

I walked across the car park and it was there.

Got into my car and it was there.

Ate my tea and it was there.

Walked the dog and it was there.

Lost my patience and it was there.

Overreacted and it was there.

Watched TV and it was there.

Went to bed and it was there.

Closed my eyes and it was there.

Opened my eyes and it was there.

Closed my eyes and it was there.

Opened my eyes and it was there.

It was everywhere, it was everyone, it was every voice, it was every sound, it was every view, it was every direction, it was everything.

It was everything.

It was everything.

And then a listening ear did appear.

A friend who wanted to hear.

And little by little, step by step it started to disappear.

I turned a corner and it wasn't there.

Opened a book and it wasn't there.

Calmed my breathing and it wasn't there.

Walked in the woods and it wasn't there

Listened to music and it wasn't there.

Grounded my feet and it wasn't there.

Climbed a hill and it wasn't there.

Drove to work and it wasn't there.

Sat at my desk and it wasn't there.

I ejected it from meetings

I removed its hands from my shoulders.

I reduced the busyness in my body.

I calmed the doubts in my mind.

I saw reality in my heart.

I discarded its mask from my face.

I strode across the car park and it wasn't there.

Leapt into my car and it wasn't there.

Savoured my tea and it wasn't there.

Played with the dog and it wasn't there.

My patience was tested and it wasn't there.

My buttons were pressed and it wasn't there.

Enjoyed the TV and it wasn't there.

Loved my family and it wasn't there.

Hugged my friends and it wasn't there.

Went to bed and it wasn't there.

Closed my eyes and it wasn't there.

Opened my eyes and it wasn't there.

It was nowhere, it was nothing.

I noticed a friend who needed an ear and I saw it there.

As we sat and shared, as we walked and talked, as we hugged and supported, I watched as it started to disappear.

I watched as they bravely and mindfully stepped on, gradually leaving it behind.

Be there, pass it on."

Letting Things Happen

23rd August 2019

For the first holiday in a decade it's been really nice to just let things happen.

Not to force things.

Not to be obsessed.

Not to try and make every second count.

Not to cram too much in.

Not to manufacture situations.

Not to try and control everything.

Not to allow cravings to disrupt.

During the week, I've been wrong, made mistakes, had my moments of doubt, my struggles, my fears, my misunderstandings, my challenges, my reminders of past battles.

But I've tried to live in each moment and enjoy what that moment brings.

To laugh, to play, to eat gorgeous food cooked by others, to share, to reminisce, to learn, to rest, to value, to recognise, to grow.

An important step – keep stepping!

Winning Hand

25th August 2019

When I woke up this morning, as I've done on most mornings for the last number of years, I did my usual three checks.

Checked on my heart, to see if that cheeky Guinness last night had caused any extra beats.

Checked on my body for anything untoward.

Checked on my mental illness to see what games it fancied playing today.

It was in need of a confidence boost, so it played:

The "Regrets" card.

The "Wasted your life" card.

The "You're not worthy" card.

The "Ruined friendships" card.

The "Missed opportunities" card.

The "Damaged your character" card.

The "Other people know more than you" card.

The "Other people are better than you" card.

I looked at my hand and, for a moment, almost admitted defeat then Facebook reminded me of a post about anxiety from 2015.

The post makes it sound like I had quite a good insight into the workings of anxiety and that I had some semblance of control. But, as the following four years have proved, I didn't really have a clue on how deep the anxiety had burrowed, how hard it would fight to keep control or how difficult it would be to be victorious.

And then, as I lay in bed this morning, I noticed a card peeking out from the sleeve of my paisley pyjamas.

Surreptitiously, I pulled the card into my hand and noticed a familiar paragraph written on it.

Without delay, I slammed the card down, trumping my opponent and ending its game.

The card?

It was the "what an ignorant, insensitive, indiscriminate, intolerable, destructive, demeaning, deadly, demonic, frustrating, frightening, fractious, frantic, time-wasting, life-changing, brain-damaging, soul-destroying little shit anxiety is and don't let anyone tell you different" card.

Better Equipped

29th August 2019

At the time I was made up, but I don't think I truly appreciated the importance of the cardiology report that I received two years ago today.

Its significance only became apparent when I started to understand the psychological impact that the years of palpitations had caused.

The test results started to dilute the fear I had of my own heart's susceptibility, a fear that fuelled increased anxiety, caused more intense palpitations and further exacerbated my distress.

The positive nature of my cardiologist's findings brought hope, breathing space, and, even though I didn't believe it at the time, a chance to start to recover but only when the psychological problems had been addressed.

Over the last few weeks, apart from a few moments, my heart has been very rhythmical, but I've noticed that at times of increased anxiety, the speed and intensity of its beats has increased.

Those moments trigger memories of how bad my heart was in those fear-riddled days and how the total preoccupation with my physical challenges together with pressures from outside influences caused massive, dangerous, and possibly life-changing reactions from my heart.

Now though, thanks to my greater awareness, understanding, and confidence, together with the breathing techniques I continually practice, I'm able to recognise the moments of anxiety early enough reducing the possibility of escalation and deal with any fallout in a more measured, focused, and less preoccupied way.

Life will always throw up times of anxiety, my heartbeat will always fluctuate but now the fear of fear itself has been reduced, thanks to the results from 2017 and the counselling that followed, I'm much better equipped to continue to live each moment more positively.

Epiphany

30th August 2019

The incredible feeling when my heart returned to its normal beat on Saturday afternoon was nothing new to me but this time its impact was more dramatic as it allowed me to realise that my heart would recover on its own, without any intervention, without any control, without any breathing techniques.

Over the last two years I've discovered that mental illnesses want us to be angry, to fight our corner, to be frustrated, to hold grudges, to feel resentment, to be jealous, to look for false positivity, to hide negatives, to "put the world to rights", to churn things over, to strive for perfection, to dwell on past challenges, and to talk about mental illness without the necessary positive support.

It hates being talked about in a supportive environment, with the correctly qualified/experienced people.

It hates forgiveness.

It hates moving on.

It hates acceptance of our limitations.

It hates real positivity.

It hates reality.

It hates realisations and it hates progress.

Which is exactly why it tries every trick to stop you in your tracks.

Access to everything it hates is in your own hands, easily attainable, and comes free of charge. You just need to take the plunge and find the courage to change direction, even if it doesn't feel like the logical, natural, or socially accepted approach.

This is not about giving up but choosing the best way to channel your energy, reframe your approach, and refocus on releasing your potential.

That wasn't just a brunch in a Church kitchen on Saturday, that was an Epiphany!

"That moment when the penny drops, and you realise that it's not all about money!"

"Being quiet is my choice; sometimes I'll choose to keep the peace, just to keep the peace!"

September 2019

Removing Control

1st September 2019

I did something yesterday that I've not been able to do for over ten years and only been able to do a very few times in my life.

I removed the control that I'd imposed on my heart.

Control that I had consciously built up over the last few years to keep things as stable as possible.

Control that I used to attempt to stop my heart going fast but inadvertently put my heart under unnatural stress and caused it to splutter like a car engine and misfire with ectopic beats.

Yesterday, as I cooked bacon and sausages at the very busy brunch, my heart rate understandably picked up, but unlike previous brunches, I consciously let my heart do what it needed to do to supply my body with the blood and energy it required.

The main reason I felt I needed to try and control my heart rate, in the past, was the fear that when it went faster it would "stick" and cause a major bout of palpitations.

After the brunch, I returned home and, because the adrenaline was still in my system, my heart continued to beat faster and then, as the stress-related hormones reduced, it naturally slowed and returned to a normal pace.

When this happens, the feeling is amazing as a warm calmness seeps through my body as the blood that has been concentrated in other parts of my body reaches the extremities and equilibrium returns.

After a couple of hours rest, we enjoyed two parties and, even after drinking three pints of Guinness (three times my usual intake), my heart continued to purr, free from the bounds that, given my previous challenges, I had placed on it.

And the possible devastating negatives had been replaced by enriching positives!

Net Became a Snare

2nd September 2019

It's strange that, for the last two years, at this time of year I've had a realisation that has changed the way I look at my mental illness.

In 2017, I recognised that through frustration and confusion, I'd been walking angrily and aggressively, pushing myself too far and bringing unnecessary tension into my body which only made my recovery even more difficult.

In 2018, I'd sussed out that my mental illness had tried to trick me and was behind all the bad things that had happened to me over the previous eight years.

At the brunch on Saturday, when I decided to remove the control that I'd placed on my heart, it was a major step and since then, as I've processed the possible benefits, it has turned into a revelation.

The control on my heart, and the associated tension it triggered, were exactly what my mental illness needed to maintain a presence in my mind, yet I thought the control was helping defeat my monster. I felt that the control, the monitoring, the breathing techniques and the awareness were necessary to allow me to progress but, in light of my discovery on Saturday, they were doing the opposite and my mental illness couldn't have been happier.

Releasing the control is not easy, it has been built up, fine-tuned, and developed over years and it has become my safety net that I have relied on numerous times to protect my heart from exploding again.

Unfortunately, the net had turned into a snare.

You Must Be Ok

4th September 2019

I recently watched a Talksport interview between James Acaster and Alan Brazil that was posted on the *Time to Change* Facebook page. The video was very powerful and enlightening.

Alan Brazil's reaction to James' mention of contacting the Samaritans and reaching out for help said so much about society's views of mental illness.

It highlighted a misconception that when you ask for help for your mental health, you must be in a really bad place, and if you don't need to contact the Samaritans, you must be ok.

When you show up for work, you must be ok.

When you socialise, you must be ok.

When you put in the extra hours, you must be ok.

When you've got a smile on your face, you must be ok.

When you're signed off with stress, but you manage to return to work, you must be ok.

When you take on that extra pressure, you must be ok.

When you keep battling on, you must be ok.

When you can't get into work but you're ok to work from home, you must be ok.

When you put projects first, you must be ok.

When you put on a brave face in a welfare check with HR, you must be ok.

When you visit the company doctor wearing a full suit of armour to hide your true challenges to protect your job, you must be ok.

When the doctor sees the anxiety and fear and desperation in your eyes, through the tiny slit that you've left exposed, and he diagnoses your mental illness … maybe you're not ok.

But because you aren't suicidal, because the diagnosis and awareness brings increased bravery, some still think that you must be ok.

My story in a nutshell: I was diagnosed with stress in 2012. A pre-existing heart condition flared up in 2013. Four years of stress-induced and anxiety-fuelled palpitations. Then finally, in 2017, it became apparent that I wasn't ok.

Thanks to the company doctor, my diagnosis changed everything and probably saved my life.

Looking back, I didn't know how powerful poor mental health could be – which led to me not taking care of myself, putting on a brave face, smiling through the pain, clothing my demons, and battling on.

Now I'm more aware of its impact, I'm more able to recognise its triggers, when it is trying to regain a foothold in my mind, when I need to take action, and the steps I can take to prevent escalation.

But also, I find that I'm constantly "topping up" my resistance, not just when I'm starting to feel low. By building up that buffer it has less chance of causing devastating flare-ups.

Gentle exercise.

Getting in touch with nature.

Taking time to rest.

Improved sleep hygiene.

Better diet.

Greater self-care.

And now my mental well-being has improved so has my physical health, and I'm able to take on more responsibility, more tasks, and work better.

Consciously Unaware

7th September 2019

A week on from my brunch-initiated epiphany and I can't believe the difference that moment has made.

I've talked before about changing my default reaction to my heart from one of brutality to one of kindness and that was a massive step but the last week has shown me that either I didn't go far enough or that I've let the fear and control back in a bit.

Even though I was more relaxed on holiday, I noticed that at times my anxiety had started to build. The week after, for various reasons, my anxiety grew and the effect on my heartbeat and my stamina was noticeable.

The decision to remove the control that I'd reinstated on my heart to combat the reinvigorated anxiety and fear changed things again.

From that moment, released from my self-imposed chains, my heart was free to beat as it needed and because it was no longer constrained, it didn't need to misfire as it tried to supply blood to my body.

As I've become accustomed to the new default reaction that is building in my heart and mind, my heart is noticeably quieter, my stamina improving, and my anxiety reducing.

It's not all been tickety boo though.

The three pints of Guinness on Saturday night and the cheeky one on Wednesday night were the perfect triggers but because I didn't think about them causing a reaction, they didn't.

Last Wednesday morning, I dreamt that I was running along a cliff and woke up with my heart racing. My brain, already seeing the benefits of the new approach, stepped in and "got it", allowing my heart to return to sinus rhythm.

Yesterday, as I implemented a project in work, all the memories of previous projects that I completed while I was struggling came to mind.

Knowing the system very well, I was fully aware of the possible problems and the challenges that I would face if those problems occurred.

As expected, there were unexpected situations to deal with and they brought the perfect opportunity for the anxiety to strike again but my reprogrammed default reaction kept things very calm, allowing me to focus on the job and deal with things appropriately.

This morning's walk on the beach was very relaxed and every so often I recognised that the awareness of my heartbeat had reduced and when I listened my brain ushered my thoughts away.

And then two contrasting words came to mind – **consciously unaware** – my new default reaction!

Be There

10th September 2019

It's World Suicide Prevention Day and, although I never had suicidal thoughts, when things were at crisis point there were times when I knew that I was one strange heartbeat, amongst the thousands of strange heartbeats, away from death or serious injury.

Even though I fought and fought to bring stability to my heart, sometimes for days on end, I can honestly say there were times when I just wanted to give in and let whatever was going to happen, happen.

It all changed on July the 4th 2017 when someone heard, in the middle of September 2017 when someone listened and since then I've made massive progress and overcome many obstacles.

I don't know where I'd be if I hadn't been heard or if I hadn't found an experienced ear to listen.

The statistics for suicides are shocking, as are the numbers of family and friends left behind to live lives without loved ones who felt they had no other option.

Be that other option.

Check up on your friends and family.

Be their change in direction.

Reduce the stigma.

Address the discrimination.

Be there.

We all have the power to play our part in increasing someone's options, lending an ear, and helping others heal.

Rebuilding

15th September 2019

Rebuilding broken relationship and friendship bridges, swept away by a wave of misunderstandings, sometimes feels like an impossible task.

A structure, that once connected two lives, lies shattered and broken along banks eroded by a torrent of misinterpretations, increasing the distance, and bringing greater instability.

The storm dies down, breathing space. Honest explanations bring clarity to the devastation. Forgiveness brings hope.

But, although the battered foundations remain intact, they lie frozen in time, unable to reconnect through fear of further escalation.

And then amongst all the noise, an impromptu meeting, unexpected and unplanned, provides opportunity for reconciliation and a hope for rebuilding relations and warming of the firm foundations.

A chance of reconnection and the reconstruction of the bridge no longer feels as daunting.

Forgive wholeheartedly, nurture hope, reach out, and, step by step, seemingly insurmountable challenges may be overcome, misunderstandings understood, differences addressed, and gaps bridged.

I'm Me

17th September 2019

At yesterday's Time to Talk session we discussed how a mental illness affects your personality and changes lifelong traits.

How it silences the chatty.

How it preoccupies the clear thinker.

How it demotivates the self-motivator.

How it irritates the calm.

How it frustrates the rational.

How it prevents growth.

How it induces cravings.

How it skews decisions.

How it damages friendships.

How it brings pressure into relationships.

How it forces you to wear a mask and work hard to appear ok, to hide what's happening inside and prevent others from noticing and offering help.

It infiltrates, it invades, it overpowers, and it subdues.

It blackens your view, it tightens its grip, it strips your power, and it paints your smile.

It removes your hope.

Looking back, even at photos from that time, I don't recognise myself, I despise what I'd become.

And then a realisation, I despise what IT had made me become.

I wasn't me, I was IT.

All the things I'd said, the decisions I'd taken, the friendships I'd damaged, the mistaken choices I'd made, the pressure I'd brought, the cravings I'd encouraged, the masks I'd worn, the irrational thoughts, and the fear of reality.

It wasn't me.

It was the terrorist in my head, the infiltrator, the invader, the foreign body, the dictator, the occupier.

And now that I've regained lost ground, removed IT from its trenches, brought calm to my mind and feel good in my own skin, I can start to repair the external damage to others and my life.

I disown those years; I write them off.

Not in a forgetful way, as if they didn't happen, but as a lesson, as an experience, an awareness raiser, a preventative measure.

I apologise to everyone affected as I try to rebuild trust, repair friendships, and rekindle relationships.

And to the home offloader, the encouraging messagers and brutally honesters, I owe you so much.

And I step on, leaving the vanquished behind.

I'm sure it will try to return, but I'm ready, I'm me!

Expose the Negativity

20th September 2019

It's strange that last night I was thinking of the positive power of facing negativity head on instead of allowing it to fester and cause internal damage, and then a post pops up from last year, when I looked back at how my counsellor helped me, and this sentence stood out:

"He knew that by exposing those negative thoughts, the positivity would return."

Our natural reaction is to push negativity to the back of our minds and almost hide it with false positivity. But that's exactly what your anxiety wants you to do because, in the deep recesses of your mind and body, unfettered and uninhibited, that negativity can flourish, cause greater negativity and further damage.

We hide the negativity for several reasons. We don't want to appear weak, we don't want to worry others, we don't want to be seen as a failure, we don't want to admit to ourselves that we are struggling, and we don't think anyone would listen.

But, as I found out last year, that was exactly what my counsellor did, he listened, he heard, he exposed the negativity, he helped me embrace it, and he showed me how to extinguish it.

Life is full of negativity, either personal or more widespread, some of the negativity can't be addressed but what my counsellor knew is that I had the power to deal with the negativity in me, not by hiding it away but by confronting it, welcoming it, talking to others who'll listen about it and then destroying it with genuine positivity.

Have you got negativity hidden away?

Is it time to be more honest with yourself and expose that negativity to a more understanding world?

It might make a world of difference.

"Hiding negative realities under false positivity is like covering hot coals with a cloth doused in petrol. Don't ignore, ignite and inflame; expose, embrace, extinguish!"

New Outlook

21st September 2019

I didn't realise it at the time, but the Wensleydale cheese moment two years ago today was a massive step.

Not only did it demonstrate that the breathing techniques worked, contrary to the doubt that I'd cast on them, but without that new approach of relaxation instead of tension, kindness instead of anger, and sensitivity instead of force, I wouldn't have been able to take the six steps agreed with my counsellor and my anxiety would still hold the upper hand.

The change of approach reframed everything I had been for the previous fifty-two years.

On the surface I've always been laid back but that change of focus made me realise that I'd been fighting a brutal war, internally, for decades.

I'd do as much as I could, cram everything in, take on new responsibilities, never slow down or listen to advice.

It was an attempt to try to make up for, and even try to rectify, the undiagnosed physical disability that blighted my life.

I'd play football and even though, after ten minutes of a sixty-minute game, my heart would explode into massive palpitations that would continue for the rest of the game, I didn't stop.

Even though my body was screaming at me, I thought I knew best, and I brutally finished the game. And then in the changing rooms, I'd brutally bring an end to the palpitations.

That brutality was in every aspect my life.

Setting up Boys' Brigade camp, refereeing football matches, playing with Jake and Sam, walking in the hills, brunches, church services, fighting viruses, getting to sleep, climbing stairs, and banging my big bass drum, all at some point triggered that brutal response.

And then there was work.

Apart from a few years, I love my job. I see it as a form of art where attention to detail is paramount and dedication and motivation to do things right prevent problems occurring later.

My brutality was evident at work too.

Taking too much on, giving everything, volunteering to get out of my depth, making changes that others had shied away from and loving having problems to solve.

All traits demonstrated by billions of people every day, but what happens when everything gets out of control? When, although you are conscious of the possible damage to business operations, you are completely unaware of the damage to yourself?

I'm in no doubt that the stoicism, stubbornness, drive, and determination that manifested from that brutality saved my bacon on several occasions and without it I wouldn't have survived my battle with mental illness.

But it was never going to solve anything, especially as my body kept breaking down time and again

Without that Wensleydale cheese moment, I wouldn't have reached my goal, overcome my anxiety, been able to talk about my challenges, helped create the Time to Talk sessions at work, which highlighted helpful podcasts and led me to discover Dr Gabor Maté and his incredible book.

A book that explained and confirmed everything that I'd discovered since that Wensleydale cheese moment.

The damage caused by the hidden stress, anxiety and brutality.

The importance of self-care.

The need to reduce the burden on my body.

The benefits of listening to my body, reducing the tension, and becoming more relaxed inside.

The book encourages exposing and accepting negativity, being more open about your challenges, allowing your body to rest, recover, and be more relaxed. And that, in return, your body will respond positively, making things easier and reducing the possibility of further, more severe problems.

But a more relaxed approach has potential setbacks in that you can feel guilty about taking things a little easier while others seem overloaded, but as my mental illness demonstrated the alternative to guilt is resentment.

Resentment that others have taken advantage of your good nature.

Resentment that you've lost years of your life to your struggles.

Resentment that your health has deteriorated.

Resentment that you've fallen behind.

Resentment that opportunities have been missed.

And as Dr Maté stated in his book, "if the choice is between guilt and resentment, choose guilt, for resentment is soul suicide."

I'd add tension, anger, force, and brutality to that as well.

My new outlook.

I've always loved Wensleydale cheese!

The Hidden Cost

28th September 2019

It's relatively easy to measure your physical weight, scales provide a numerical representation in various easily monitored measurements.

This allows action to be taken to address overweight or underweight situations.

The same can't be said for psychological weight. It's impossible to measure or represent emotional baggage as an obvious numerical value and this is the crux of the problem.

Even though the effects of a mental illness can be recognised, i.e. by changes in demeanour, reaction, communication, sense of humour, and even walking style etc., there is no mechanism to quantify the demands that the mental illness places on someone's shoulders or how it reduces their capabilities, social standing, focus, dedication, concentration, and confidence.

And, in a world that relies on visible statistics, because it can't be quantified or measured, many view the consequences of psychological problems as non-existent.

We can measure time off sick caused by mental illness, that is recognised and admitted by those struggling, and this has been calculated to cost the UK economy £1.4 billion a year, but, from my experiences, this figure is grossly underestimated.

Over 40% of employees are reluctant to disclose that their time off sick is due to a problem with their mental health, preferring to blame a physical or viral illness instead. This very fact only serves to inflate the £1.4 billion cost.

But, as the effects of a mental illness are difficult to quantify, it is almost impossible to gauge how many hours/days/weeks/months are lost to those who attend work but, because of their invisible struggles, demonstrate poor productivity, lack of concentration, pre-occupation, brain-fog and irritability whilst being victims of reactive and insufficient support, misunderstandings, poor management and being side-lined because they are deemed weak or unable to cope.

Now that I've overcome the problems that I faced, I can look back and see how bad I was during my struggles.

Now that I'm becoming more involved in decision making, I can see how much I've missed, how far I've fallen behind and how catching up is challenging and time-consuming.

Now I'm more stable, I can begin to quantify how I performed when my mental illness was at its most severe.

I honestly believe that, during that time, I was working at between 25% and 40% of my available capacity when compared to how I performed before my mental illness took hold and to how I'm delivering now.

The lost productivity, the cost of mistakes or poor design, the extra workload, and pressure placed on colleague's shoulders and the damage to relationships can never be measured but to lose between 60% and 75% of capacity has to result in a cost being incurred that further increases the measurable £1.4 billion already calculated.

A solution to reduce the cost of mental illness to businesses is to provide a culture of effective, pro-active and valued support. To create a structure that allows management and colleagues the skills to recognise possible mental health problems at the earliest opportunity and to be able to "step in" and signpost colleagues to professional help, if required.

As my battles and the length and challenging nature of my recovery have shown, proactive recognition and support is essential in reducing cost and improving culture.

Reactive care is too late and vastly more expensive.

Big steps have already been taken where I work but we still need to keep stepping!

"Forgiveness is an art; some find it easy while others need practice. Some will see its beauty, others will not. But don't be dismayed, keep practicing, for the real beauty lies in the eyes of the artist!"

"Don't be envious and jealous of the possessions of others, be happy and satisfied that you've made a success of your choice to take a different path and chose different priorities."

October 2019

Be Honest

1st October 2019

Post from 1st October 2016:

Find strength in your confidence, love in your friends. Know that you can't always be perfect, it's ok to show weakness and to ask for help! Even the strong need a hand to get along!

Three years ago today I must have been feeling stronger. But looking back, I was masking the unrecognised, unknown, and misunderstood negatives with false positivity and putting on a brave face.

In reality, my confidence was paper thin, the protective walls that I'd erected were made of jelly and my foundations were built on sand. Behind the front were several bouts of palpitations a week, numerous ectopics, and a thinly veiled fear of the future.

In the first six months of 2017, the negatives burst through my fragile defences bringing the unstable house of cards crashing down and rendering the positivity useless.

Given that I'd been feeling better at the end of 2016, the events of 2017 pushed me down to my lowest level of despair but, thankfully, they also led to help being provided which allowed me to rebuild my confidence into a wad of knowledge, reinforce the walls with bricks, and resit my foundations on rock.

The negatives were exposed, the positivity genuine, the mask removed, and palpitations reduced to nearly zero.

False strength masks pain, soldiering on, battling through, only serves to hide the truth. Scared to show weakness, frightened to ask for help, an unexpected hand reaches out and slowly the light returns.

Even the strong need a hand to get along.

Be honest with yourself.

At the Crossroads
4th October 2019

Post from 4th October 2017:

I love it when my brain wakes me up in the middle of the night because it's analysed everything that is going on in my life at the moment, come up with the perfect approach and was too excited to wait until dawn to tell me about it.

Yesterday I signed a pact with my brain, heart, and soul to NEVER let anything or anyone affect the wonderful way I'm feeling at the moment.

Thanks to my brain's night shift, I now have something I've been searching for over the last few months, a plan to bring closure in a calm, controlled, and constructive way.

And I, like my brain, heart, and soul, couldn't be more excited!

On the evening of the 3rd of October 2017, I stood at a crossroads. Turn left and face confrontation, escalation, and extended damage from my struggles or turn right and take control, employ forgiveness, and move closer to closure of my battles.

The events of the previous three months had led me to that point.

People had been brought into my life to help me and, through their guidance and instruction, I'd made progress towards the start of my recovery. But even though I'd been placed at that decision point, I had to choose which way to turn.

I knew how things would be if I turned left. It was a well-trodden path that had been explored by many before me but, as with my ablation in 2004, I didn't have clue what would happen if I took the opposite, less well known, and less understood path.

Turning left seemed the socially accepted way to turn, to face things with more anger, to raise tensions, to fight my corner, and never to give in.

Turning right seemed submissive; giving in, rolling over, and losing out.

And then, as this memory from 2017 outlines, the voice in my sleep spoke to me, giving me a glimpse of a better solution and showing me the way that I couldn't see, down the path seldom trod.

The next morning, revitalised by the different approach that had reframed the impending meeting, I was ready.

To remove the confrontation, I carried only a bottle of water and my phone, with the words written in the early hours crafted and stored away. I wore a white t-shirt. I arrived early with a cheery greeting. I was focused, cool, calm, and clinical.

I stood my ground, non-aggressively.

I took control, surprisingly.

I directed, inventively.

I educated, enlighteningly.

I found closure, gracefully.

I finished the day on the 4th of October, ready for the five days of recovery steps that I'd been planning for weeks.

But, the following day, the anxiety that had built up over the previous three days, showed itself in a form of palpitations that would last for hours and threatened to scupper the first step agreed with my counsellor. Thankfully, using the techniques he'd shown me, I was able to take that first step unscathed.

Only this morning, two years later when I was recalling the event of 2017 and given the subsequent reaction in my heart, I wondered what would have happened if I turned left at that crossroads, if the voice hadn't directed me in the night and the tension, the anxiety, the resentment, and the bitterness had overflowed.

That voice, that choice, and that path, which may have saved my life, certainly changed my destiny.

Are you at a crossroads, finding the choice difficult, wanting to head down the failed path of confrontation?

Take your time, think hard, listen to your inner voice, turn away from your demons, and see what lies in the other direction. Choose wisely!

Hardest First Step

6th October 2019

A mental illness wants to make the distance you need to cover to recover as big and as challenging as possible.

It will try to keep you in your darkness, to erect obstacles in your way, to escalate your thoughts and worries and tie you down with total preoccupation.

As you yearn to return to your former self or rekindle your dreams, the sheer enormity of that journey fills you with dread and you choose what has become the new norm and stay put.

As the saying goes, "the first step is the hardest" and, given the size of the chasm that stands before you, such a small step feels pointless.

So, you don't take it, putting it off through fear, uncertainty, and the worthlessness that your mental illness has made you feel.

Your mental illness keeps you stuck, static, and under its control.

By blackening your view, it masks the reality that surrounds you, knowing that if you see it, you might have the motivation to take that important first step.

The first step only needs to be small and within your capabilities.

Regular gentle exercise through a local wood gets you in back touch with nature.

Prioritising self-care improves your diet and sleep hygiene providing quality time to rest.

Little steps forward that appear inconsequential and too minor to reduce the severity of the burdens that lie behind your mental illness but, through their simplicity and ease, provide breathing space. Space to refocus your thoughts, reframe your challenges, lighten your view, and commence your recovery.

As you cautiously step on, and you feel more confident to remove the blinkers imposed on you, your view widens, and a more positive reality starts to appear.

But even when you've taken hundreds of steps and you've begun to confidently pick up pace, setbacks will occur. Attempts to derail your progress.

Each negative impediment threatens to scupper your recovery and darken your newly sparked light.

However, despite the knocks, you must continue to step on, undeterred if a little shaken, towards that light. A light which maybe is slightly dimmed but still flickers with newly discovered hope.

Your determination pays off and the intensity of your light grows brighter, the stride in your step more confident, the distance on your journey greater, the previously unreachable gap reduces, and, most importantly, the underlying burdens less negative.

You move from the wood to the forest, gradually increasing the incline of your climb.

Faster, more assured, you reach greater heights. The setbacks still come but now their impact is minimal.

You sense victory.

You replace tension with acceptance, anger with forgiveness.

You march on until suddenly, with your aggressor defeated, you don't need to march anymore, and you can relax, soak in the scenery, reduce your pace, and live a life that you never dreamt existed.

And it all started with that first step.

Two years ago today I took my first step, by walking up a sand dune, and yesterday I reaped its benefits.

Step and then keep stepping!

Genuine Positivity

10th October 2019

On days like today, it's always encouraging to see the surge of posts that talk about mental health. Every post, comment and like plays their part in further reducing the stigma and normalising the subject.

Many of the posts pledge positivity for the days, weeks, months, and years ahead and negativity, in the majority of posts, is never dared to be mentioned.

But I think it's even more important to say on these hashtag days that a life lived with total positivity is impossible, counterproductive, and, in the most complex situations, very dangerous.

Life is full of negatives, that's the reality.

To say that is not to be a doom and gloom merchant but to recognise that shit happens.

People get sick, jobs are lost, accidents happen, dreams aren't always fulfilled, marriages breakup, and friendships end.

Pulling on positive pants, painting on a false smile, and pretending that everything in your garden is rosy doesn't stop negative things happening and when (not if) they do, the shock of unpreparedness can cause greater fallout as the positivity is instantly flushed away. And the fall from false heights is more devastating.

I've mentioned before about how I struggled when my counsellor warned me to "expect setbacks" during my recovery.

He told me so I'd be prepared for the inevitable negatives that were guaranteed to occur.

Armed with this prediction, I was able to accept and even embrace the negative moments when they occurred. This didn't diminish the power of positivity, in fact it expanded its scope and brought greater freedom.

False, forced positivity can have a devastating negative effect on someone battling to recover from a mental illness, especially those who, under the surface, are very vulnerable.

Being genuinely positive is a major factor in recovering from a mental illness but this needs to be balanced with recognition that negative situations are all part of life's rich tapestry.

They should be openly expected, not hidden behind a flimsy, tense front but treated with strength, kindness, and sensitivity!

Positive steps from life's negativity.

From Both Sides

12th October 2019

"I've a bad back that is making me depressed, and the depression is making my back worse."

Three options –

1. Pain relief and physio for the back but nothing for the depression

2. Nothing for the back but antidepressants for the depression

3. Pain relief, physio, and support for the back pain and counselling and support for the depression

Option one may relieve the pain but it would only be short-term relief before the untreated depression and anxiety caused another physical reaction.

Option two may reduce the symptoms from the depression but the untreated back pain would counteract any reduction.

Option three is the holistic approach. Treatment to reduce the back pain and determine the root cause, which in turn reduces the depression and anxiety. In tandem with deep psychological help to expose the reasons, background, and triggers for the depression, to provide techniques and assistance during recovery and a manageable goal to attain.

Only option three works but because many GPs and physicians don't see the connection between the mind and the body, they choose one of the other simpler, less expensive (on the surface) options.

Take the back pain and replace it with heart disease and that's my battle.

If the Occupational Health Doctor had only prescribed a cardio check and drugs to stop the palpitations when they occurred, the untreated mental illness would have continued to destroy my life.

If he'd given me antidepressants and no cardio support, the deep-rooted psychological problems would never have been exposed and they would have continued to trigger more devastating palpitations rendering the antidepressants useless and causing greater heart disease.

Only by recognising the connection between the mind and the body and treating both at the same time could have worked.

I'm so glad the Occupational Health Doctor took option three and changed my life, from both angles!

Winning the Battles

17th October 2019

It's difficult to believe that something you can't see, can't touch, can't smell and that only you may be able to hear, can have such a devastating effect on your mental and physical well-being.

At its early stages, you may not even recognise its presence but slowly, quietly, and slyly it eats away in the dark, triggering minor reactions and remaining relatively unnoticed and its impact is dismissed, out of hand.

Gradually and methodically, it starts to gain increased control, remoulding your thoughts and altering your instinctive responses to everyday situations.

The invasion gains pace and more control is lost, increasing the severity of the reactions, initiating physical symptoms and further expanding its reach and impact.

Anxiety is very smart and, if allowed free rein without proactive recognition, it is very difficult to escape from its clutches.

It will fight until the very end to try to continue to influence your life, and make you feel that progress is impossible, even if you've taken great strides towards its destruction.

The first steps were to see, to touch, to smell my assailant, to recognise its impact, and to play it at its own game, slowly, quietly, slyly, and methodically increasing control of my own mind and regaining lost ground.

You may feel the battle will never be won but by taking small, meaningful, and achievable steps, whilst considering your own personal circumstances, not over stretching yourself and expecting negative setbacks, progress can be made, a positive resolution reached or important life improving changes realised.

Right to Choose

18th October 2019

When friends or family members choose to do something that frustrates or angers you, it can cause resentment, bitterness, and friction, which can result in long-standing repercussions and fallout.

In some cases, the choice will be taken out of spite and your reaction needs to be as measured as possible, to protect your mental well-being.

However, in most cases, the decision will have been made based on the individual's current circumstances. They may not want to or be able to explain their reasons and, understandably, feel no need to justify their actions.

Regardless of the reasons behind the decision, the resentment and bitterness you feel will still build up, but the only thing you can control is how you react to this situation.

It's worth noting that it's ok and, in fact, healthy, to express your anger in a right and beneficial way. Bottling the anger up will lead to further complications to your health.

However, trying to change their decision, especially without being aware of the other person's current circumstances, will only escalate the bad feeling, cause greater fallout and further disconnection.

Conversely, by recognising that the other person has the right to choose their own path, based on their circumstances and requirements, helps you to start to understand the possible reasons for their choice and allows forgiveness for the previously disputed decision.

The recognition, understanding and forgiveness serves to reduce the intensity of your anger, resentment, bitterness, and frustration, de-escalating or even preventing friction between you and the other person and keeping the door open to the possibility of re-engagement in the future.

I've been wrestling with this for some time, it feels good to finally rationalise and articulate my thoughts.

I wrote this quote some years back, but it's still relevant today –

"A true friend just wants their friends to be happy, loved, and safe … no matter the circumstances and distance that may keep them apart."

Accepting Bad Feelings

29th October 2019

When I was struggling, the night times were so hard.

As soon as my head hit the pillow, my heart would start to jump which raised my anxiety and made sleep incredibly difficult. Then, after finally managing to get to sleep, I'd be woken up in the early hours and my mind would start to race and be filled with anxiety-driven thoughts.

The lack of sleep would then impact me the following day, causing my heart to react and then, even though I was very tired, sleep would be even more challenging the following night.

Although it wasn't one single thing that allowed me to break that cycle, the main change I made was to reprogram my brain to react differently when it started to race.

I'd already started to change the way I reacted when my heart went strange during the day, and gradually I was able to start to use the same technique to improve my sleep hygiene.

You may wonder how you can reprogram your thoughts and reactions but by consciously deciding a different approach can make that possible.

When you wake up, you feel angry and become tense, this then causes your brain to release stress hormones to fight those feelings. These hormones naturally make you feel more aware and alert and that wakes you up even more, causing your mind to start to race, making sleep impossible.

The technique I used to help control my heartbeat changes the approach from anger and tension to acceptance and sensitivity. This approach, instead of releasing the stress hormones, triggers a calmer reaction.

It may sound strange to welcome, embrace, and accept bad feelings but by triggering that calmer reaction, you are able to realise that you can't deal with those feelings at that moment and it's ok to leave them until the morning.

It takes practice, time, and patience and can be frustrating to start with but gradually, as you continue to use this approach, you find that you are starting to fall asleep sooner even when you wake up in the night.

It's also something you can practice during the day, as I did with my heart.

When situations happen that make you feel angry, frustrated, or resentful, check how you react and decide to react in a more accepting, sensitive, and forgiving way.

The angry and tense reactions are food and drink to your anxiety, the different approach reduces that anger and tension, brings calm to your body and mind and reality to your thoughts that are exaggerated by the night.

I can't recommend this approach enough. I still wake up in the early hours and my brain starts to trigger those thoughts but then it remembers the mindful approach, it accepts the thoughts have occurred and then quietly silences them until the morning, when things seem easier to deal with.

"If someone isn't prepared to change for the better, the least you can do is not let them change you for the worse."

"Don't tell me you care, show me."

November 2019

Too Nice

2nd November 2019

I was once told that I was too nice.

It was seen by the other person as a negative trait that should be reduced in favour of a more selfish, self-centred, hard-faced, and aggressive approach to life and other people.

At the time, my psyche said, "No, that's not me!" but looking back over the last decade, I realise there was an element of truth in what was said.

I now recognise that my nice, can-do, selfless attitude was a major contributor to my mental illness.

The putting others first, the never giving in, the self-motivation, the plate spinning and never saying no all led to me being taken advantage of, being left exposed, and under supported.

Until, even though I couldn't vocalise the word, my body said no for me.

I heard on the radio the other day that there's a degree of truth in the fact that, due to their nature, the more selfish, self-centred people are less likely to experience poor mental health.

The question is why?

Is it because they don't care about the feelings of others, so they don't get involved in the detrimental challenges that those relationships can bring?

Is it because they are so focused on their own needs that they have difficulty in engaging in the struggles of those around them?

Or is it because they can recognise when they are being taken advantage of and say no, even if maybe too abruptly, thereby protecting themselves from psychological harm?

But surely, as is the case in the majority of life, there must be a happy medium.

An approach that doesn't bring either extreme.

A way that won't damage relationships from over self-protection but brings an awareness that prevents people taking advantage yet allows relationships and friendships to be nurtured and grow.

An unexpected by-product of a struggle with mental illness that will see many false dawns, many confidence builders, many setbacks, and many protective celebrations.

And that can bring about that "happy medium", of continued care and consideration for others and their circumstances, while increasing awareness of those trying to take advantage.

Together with a new view on a word, that when used in abrupt, closed, angry, resentful, and bitter ways can be deeply damaging, but when said with understanding, kindness, sensitivity, and forgiveness can bring healing, greater connection, and better relationships.

"No, I won't!" or "No, I'm sorry, to protect myself, I can't. Let's work on this together."

An aspiration? An unreachable utopia? Or a genuinely, achievable life?

Brand New Me

13th November 2019

Post from 13th November 2017:

When someone finally shines a light on their poor handling of your past, use it to illuminate their failings rather than cast a shadow on your successes.

#malarky

This status from two years ago summed up a very difficult day during my recovery from mental illness.

Even though I'd finished my counselling and was better equipped to deal with situations like this, my recovery was still in its infancy and all the hard work could easily have been ruined.

The word "Malarky'" encapsulates so much from that day, but to expand things a little, I wrote this poem when I was out with Coco this morning –

"The evidence lay before me, scribed in black and white,

Long years of indifference finally came to light.

False assumptions, blame pinned on me,

The attempts to derail my progress, very clear to see.

My blood boiled, my heart began to race,

But I was seeing a different view, in a better place.

My new technique, my calmer thought,

Now I was judge and jury, laughing out of court.

Onward I walked, and higher I climbed,

Doubts, fear, and misjudgements firmly left behind.

Setbacks defeated, my confidence increasing,

Heart stability restoring, so I kept on stepping.

I still can't quite fathom, a motive for that day,

Forgiveness released the burdens, as I continued on my way.

Past bitterness and resentment, confined to history,

A brighter horizon revealed, a brand new me."

Bodied

18th November 2019

That moment when my mental illness tries to use my very enjoyable weekend away to regain a foothold and gets absolutely bodied by my brain!

Keep stepping!

Be Your PB

22nd November 2019

Another learning opportunity this week.

On Monday, after our overcast but very enjoyable weekend away in the Lakes, I was dealing with the Post Break Blues while the sun shone in the Lakes and friends were sharing their photos of their on-going trips to far and wide.

Seizing on these frustrations, my mental illness tried to regain a foothold and instigate a comeback. For a few hours, the attempt to derail my recovery started to affect my mood, until my focused brain recognised the culprit and quietened its noise, reconciled the reason and restored the disturbed equilibrium.

The moment my brain bodied my mental illness was a major boost as it reinforced the steps I'd taken and brought reassurance that my techniques were still in control, even after a slight slip down a few steps.

Then, while I was watching *24 hours in A&E*, a patient who had just had an Implantable Cardioverter Defibrillator (ICD) fitted, following heart problems when he was running, was told by the doctors to push his heart as hard as he could, and the patient responded –

"I'd rather die doing what I enjoy than sit on a couch eating crisps."

A very commendable and admirable approach but also very dangerous and it highlighted to me how society always seems to deal only in extremes.

Triathlon or couch potato.

Overweight or too skinny.

Rich or poor.

But, in reality, life is not that black and white, and we all live on our own unique and individual spectrums.

We all live different lives, with disparate challenges, circumstances, relationships, situations, and backgrounds.

Lives which create personal spectrums of varying sizes, differing number and severity of steps, unpredictable difficulties, and life-changing opportunities.

The position on our spectrum is fluid and, given situations that naturally occur, it's ok to fall back a few steps and, when the time is right, start to make forward progress again.

Recognising this fluidity, and mindfully applying this realisation to everyday life, it's possible to quieten the irritating white noise created by others, to reduce the weight of trivial burdens and distinguish between insignificant, inconsequential issues and significant, important concerns.

This recognition brings space, time, and capacity to handle the major life-changing challenges that life throws at us with greater assuredness and conviction, instead of being bogged down by the time-wasting, space-consuming weight of life's trivialities.

By embracing your current situation and finding enjoyment and fulfilment in each moment, you can discover gratification and stimulation in even the menial and repetitive tasks, opening a whole new view on your position on your spectrum, reducing the pressure and expectation from a skewed society, respecting the fluidity of life and bringing a new outlook on your well-being.

Contrary to society's extremes, just because you may never be able to complete a triathlon doesn't mean you are a couch potato.

If you are struggling and the fear of failure looms again, keep stepping in whatever way is manageable by you.

Take care and, if beating your Personal Best is sometimes impossible, being your Personal Best is always achievable!

A Walk in the Park

24th November 2019

Given the nature and sensitivity of the subject, talking and posting about mental illness can cause misunderstandings and unexpected reactions. A single word can trigger unintended pain, a misinterpreted phrase instigates unanticipated consternation and even possible confrontation.

So, we choose the safer, less damaging option and decide it's best not to talk about mental health problems at all.

And, by doing so, we play right into the hands of the very thing we want to challenge, the stigma that surrounds this devastating, socially excluding subject.

Which in turn further increases our frustration, possibly causes even greater disconnection with our friends and family and intensifies our invisible symptoms.

My post on Friday is a case in point, but it served several purposes.

It allowed me to articulate, in narrative writing, what I'd experienced and learned last week.

It kept the easily abandoned conversation going and, hopefully, continued to educate and enlighten others who either may be on a similar journey or are unaware of the dangers of this emotive subject.

It instigated valued dialogue with good friends that brought a degree of clarity to my thoughts and further expanded the scope of understanding.

And it highlighted the need to keep posting, to keep talking, to keep challenging, to keep reaching the parts that don't want to be reached and to keep pushing back against this very resilient adversary.

For years, I was fearful of myself and of the invisible and unrecognised assailant that caused so much deep-rooted, life-changing, time-wasting, and life-threatening damage.

But now, the fear has been reduced, the resultant confidence has allowed me to address issues that were causing my anxiety, fear, and physical symptoms and, by keeping posting and talking about this emotive subject, quite literally the boot is on the other foot and the need to keep stepping even more important.

The route ahead is full of possible difficulties and pitfalls but compared to the crater-strewn, severely undulating road that lies behind me, it's a walk in the park.

Breaking Habits

26th November 2019

It's perfectly natural to be stoic at various parts of your life.

Times that need inner strength, drive, and determination to carry on, regardless of the situation, consequences, or adverse effects that may be instigated.

My battles with Congenital Heart Defects (CHD) have led to decades of stoicism as I journeyed through significant episodes of my life.

1. Birth to Open Heart Surgery

2. Unmanageable palpitations post OHS

3. Brutal control of undiagnosed heart defect

4. Post-ablation calm

5. Stress-induced and anxiety-driven arrhythmia

6. Recovery from fear and mental illness

Only in the last two months have I realised how much this stoicism has influenced my life.

How it has helped me survive and, apparently, mitigate my struggles and strife.

How its brutality has influenced my approach to numerous situations and framed my views and reactions.

At the start of October this year, with the help of support from a Facebook group for those living with CHD, I recognised that the stoicism that had helped me through so much in the past was now holding me back. That it was no longer fit for purpose, had outlived its effectiveness and, only today, did I realise exactly what it had been hiding.

Slowly, during my recovery from mental illness over the last few years, fifty-four years of stoicism has been peeled away to reveal hidden empathetic characteristics long disguised by half a century of toils, conflict, and fragile existence.

Compassion and understanding formed by the close connection with my empathetic centre, my heart, a direct consequence of living with congenital heart defects.

Then, after a simple Google search, the real effects of being stoic for so long become evident and the true negative synonymous side-effects of this powerful word became clearer –

Aloof

Apathetic

Detached

Impassive

Long-suffering

Unemotional

Tense

Forced

Suddenly, questions that until now have laid unnoticed, could start to be exposed and addressed.

Why do I need to carry on being stoic?

What purpose does it serve?

Is it holding me back?

How will reducing my stoicism transform my life?

The answers lie in the antonyms of the word –

Caring

Concerned

Emotional

Feeling

Interested

Responsive

Ease

Focused

Empathetic

So why do we hold on to such a negative trait and continue to be stoic, long after its usefulness has expired, and its influence becomes more of a burden than a benefit?

Are we frightened to let go of the very thing that has kept us alive?

Do we think that by relinquishing its strength will make us weak in the eyes of others?

Are we holding on to it to allow us to continue to complete tasks that we have loyally fulfilled for years but that are now physically damaging us through unnecessary tension and fortitude?

I'm quickly discovering that the reduction in stoicism actually makes me feel more alive, stronger, more in control. It reduces physical symptoms, and I feel able to lay down tiring responsibilities that my body can now longer perform with the same ease as it did in previous years.

And all those advantageous antonyms are opening up a new view on how I can live my life, free from the millstones and negativity associated with being stoic.

And the empathy that lay covered and disguised for many, many years brings benefits that far outweigh the very thing that kept it hidden.

Is it time to lay down responsibilities in your life that are causing you pain and discomfort but, because you've stoically and loyally performed those tasks for years, you feel guilty for relinquishing your duties?

There's no need to feel any guilt, there's no need to continue to feel that pain, there's no need to bravely and stoically fulfil damaging and unnecessary roles.

There's a new view to be seen, a new tension-reduced life to lead and a new response to be nurtured.

Reduce the stoicism, believe me, it's no longer helping, and the time has come to put you first and regain connection with your empathetic self. And that will change everything and bring a new perspective on what's really important in life.

Important Step

30th November 2019

Following on from my post about reducing the stoicism in our lives that suppresses so much anger and emotion, a friend shared an article on Facebook yesterday.

The article gives us two choices –

Continue to stoically "exert control. Maintaining iron-will control over my every emotion. But this only works for so long before the emotions leak out and erupt like a dormant volcano."

Or

By giving those negative feelings "a voice, I allowed them their day in the sun. I knew that by releasing them, it didn't mean that they would linger or stick around longer than I needed them to.

I just felt them and gave them the space to be released, so I could pass through it. I allowed them to do their healing work by owning that they are there. Yes, I'm still sad. I'm still grieving. I feel lonely and in need of love.

But they no longer have power over me. Because I'm feeling them now instead of repressing them, numbing them, or trying to control them."

A big but important step!

"*Prejudice - to prejudge someone's ways and actions without first hearing their story.*"

"*Don't drain my generosity, without helping me refuel.*"

December 2019

Unexpected Realisation

6th December 2019

Driving home from work last night, thinking about my fellow Congenital Heart Defect patients who had been sharing their celebrations of forty and fifty years since their Open-Heart Surgery, when an unexpected realisation hit me.

I've always recognised the work that went into preparing my body for surgery, the visible chest scar is a constant reminder, and the post care, but until last night, in the forty-six years and seven months since that day in the technologically poor 1970s, I've never thought of this…

My heart, the very empathetic centre of my being, has been physically touched and held by the hands of another human being.

Initially, as I drove down the A565, that thought freaked me out as I squirmed and shouted in the driver's seat. But soon that initial reaction was replaced with appreciation that those hands weren't just any hands.

They were hands of skill, kindness, tenderness, compassion, dedication, dexterity, and love.

All traits that change, shape, save, enhance, and transform lives.

I owe the hands of Professor Dr David Ian Hamilton FRCS so much, and I'll try to continue to repay this great man in any way I can.

Talking Can Change Your Life

14th December 2019

As I parked near Freshfield Station this morning, I noticed three men stood behind a car. It looked like dodgy deal was going on!

Then, as I put Coco's muzzle on in the back of my car, one of the men approached me and asked me if I wanted a free poo bag dispenser and a card from the Samaritans.

We chatted for a few minutes about how my mental illness was recognised by the Occupational Health Doctor and how my life was changed by talking and being heard.

Ironically, last night I lay in bed listening to my heart purring away. I then realised that it's been over three months since my last noticeable bout of palpitations, and how much my life has changed since I talked, someone listened, and I was heard.

After shaking the man by the hand, I walked on with the other things that have helped me on my journey. Gently increased exercise, getting closer to nature, and having a buddy to walk alongside me.

And, as the card said, "Talking can change your life!"

Changing Life-Long Traits

25th December 2019

In 2014, soon after the worst bouts of palpitations in my life and when each moment was a constant battle for survival, I decided to remove as many of the probable causes from my life as possible.

Alcohol and caffeine have never played a significant part in my life so reducing their intake to zero was relativity straightforward and, in their place, I increased my levels of exercise by taking on a yearlong walking challenge.

Removing the stimulants had a slight positive effect but because the exercise was forced and became a burden, that improvement was negated, and the symptoms kept occurring.

In 2018, when I was feeling more settled psychologically, I gradually increased the levels of alcohol and caffeine and, after recognising the negative effects from forced exercise, I started to walk more relaxed. And, thankfully, the palpitations didn't reoccur.

This brought an interesting thought into my mind and, given my recent discoveries about the damage caused by life-long traits, such as stoicism and unfettered self-perseverance, a chance to uncover the real culprit behind my challenges.

Last night, for only the second time in a decade, to test my theory, I enjoyed a brandy while staying relaxed and fearless, and because there was no reaction in my heart, my suspicions were confirmed.

It was never the alcohol or caffeine or the forced exercise that caused the physical reaction, it was the fear that I had about the consequences of my actions. And that fear led to an increase in the underlying cause of my troubles, that has been a constant during the last 10 years … tension.

As I discovered through mindfulness and the work of Dr Gabor Maté, increased, poorly managed tension leads to secondary suffering, anxiety, depression, more tension, and the vicious circle is complete.

On the surface, I've always appeared laid back and not tense but, as I've stripped back the life-long habits that are a result of happenings in my life, I've realised that those characteristics have been the instigators of the unseen and unrecognised tension. You could say that I'm to blame for letting that tension build up, but those traits were not created by choice but by circumstance.

And now, as a new decade approaches, it's time to take the next step and resolve to reduce the instances of that tension and the conflict that it brings, both internally to me and externally to others.

Maybe the biggest challenge I've had to face during my recovery.

Try to find time to relax, rest, recover, and recharge during the festive period!

Cheers!

Harnessing the Power of Your Mind

29th December 2019

I noticed last night, during a lovely Italian with Kay's family, how relaxed I was and how that allowed me to engage better in the conversations.

This was in complete contrast to how I've felt in previous situations, especially in recent years, when I would have to force everything.

Force myself to socialise, to eat, to control my heart that would react as my food was digesting, to force my anxious mind to listen to the conversations and to force my engagement with those around me.

All that forcing affected my speech and my confidence which in turn made me quiet and appear rude and ignorant.

But last night, the force was replaced by focus.

Savouring every mouthful, tasting every drop, engaging in conversation, and being the me that had been hidden for so long.

Fancy a New Year's resolution that will gradually change your life?

When faced with a decision on how to react, mindfully bring kindness and sensitivity to the situation, even if that is painful, and reduce the anxiety by consciously breathing out the tension and resistance.

And you'll begin to notice that the disabling force is gradually replaced by enriching focus.

And you'll start to harness the real positive power of your mind.

Take That Step

31st December 2019

In 2018, I concentrated on re-building my confidence by gradually increasing my physical activity. My focus was on completing the forty-five-peak challenge for Heartbeat and reaching the goal agreed with my counsellor.

During 2019, I decided to reduce the pressure on my body, consolidate the progress I'd made, to start to give attention to the psychological side of my recovery and look to change the mental health provision at work.

Since 2017, I'd been slowly discovering the power of mindfulness and the part it had played in allowing me to reach my goal and complete my challenge. Things took a slight change of direction when Jake bought me a book for Christmas, *The Subtle Art of Not Giving a F****. This brought a more selfish approach to mindfulness; the art of self-care, reassessing my values and priorities, setting manageable and achievable goals and not getting obsessed with the insignificant parts of life.

At the start of February, with the support of the new Senior Management Team at work, I helped start monthly Time to Talk sessions at work. One of the first topics was podcast recommendations and this made me aware of Dr Rangan Chatterjee. The first podcast I listened to was with Danny Penman who described his experiences with the same mindfulness technique that I had been practicing.

I then picked another podcast at random and listened with amazement as Dr Gabor Maté discussed the power that childhood trauma has on your adult life. I then bought Dr Maté's book, "When the Body Says No: The Cost of Hidden Stress", and slowly the jigsaw pieces started to fall into place, but it would be another few months before I fully understood the impact of these revelations.

Last October, a Facebook friend shared photos from a conference about Congenital Heart Defects and their impact in Adult life. This led me to joining the Somerville Foundation Facebook group which further explained the life-long trauma that is associated with the challenges of living with CHD.

This was the final piece of the jigsaw as I realised the massive part that stoicism and stubbornness had played in my life.

How it had helped me survive my early years of massive undiagnosed and uncontrollable palpitations.

How it had made me the master of hiding things and ignoring the signals from my body and soldering on.

How this had allowed the dark shadows of mental illness to build until my body said no as the hidden stress caused an explosion in my heart.

How it had given me the strength and perseverance to survive four years of disabling and dangerous palpitations.

How it was holding me back and was no longer fit for purpose.

In 2009, I was looking forward to the next decade with massive optimism, but I was unaware and stoically naïve of what lay ahead. As 2019 comes to an end, I'm back in the same position but now I'm more aware of the potential of psychological problems and how to recognise and manage them.

And I've realised that the stoicism and stubbornness is a result of my childhood trauma and that self-care, openness, honesty, and support (both physical and psychological) are more important.

When it was suggested that I have six weeks of CBT Counselling, my stoicism tried to convince me that I didn't need it. That I would be seen as a failure. I would appear weak. It would be embarrassing and a retrograde step.

The stoicism was wrong as it was the best step I'd taken on my road to recovery and everything that it has revealed.

In 2020, if support is offered to help you on your journey either physical or psychological, accept the offer, embrace the opportunity, don't feel embarrassed, weak or a failure, take that step, it may possibly change your life.

"It's strange how life decisions become easier when you've been shown and seen the bigger picture ... not seen it yet? Open your eyes, take off your blinkers and look around, you're surrounded!"

"Don't judge me on the actions, the words, and the opinions of others, they is them and I is me, the difference is plain to see!"

January 2020

Influencing Your Future

2nd January 2020

"Don't look back, you're not going that way."

A popular motivational phrase but, although I agree with the sentiment, it has never really sat right in my mind, this morning I worked out why.

To me, the phrase is encouraging us to ignore our past because, obviously, we can't change what has happened. However, by disregarding our historic ordeals we are missing a vitally important part in shaping our future.

Putting it bluntly, it is impossible to ignore your past.

There are too many triggers, memories, and reminders in everyday life that, without correctly targeted focus and mindful management of past situations, will repeatedly trip us up and continue to affect what lies ahead.

Here's an example.

Every morning, I'll prepare Coco for her first walk of the day.

As I put on her harness, click on her lead, and gently strap the muzzle on her face, I'm immediately reminded of the situation that brought about her life-long Control Order.

This trigger then brings into focus the inadequacies of the other owner in controlling their dog, which in turn prompts thoughts of the preventable failures that led to my mental illness and the bitterness, anger, resentment, and frustration that is associated with both historical situations.

Every day, as I look into Coco's sad eyes while she patiently accepts the confines of her muzzle, this totally unrelated thought process is initiated.

And every day, because I've looked back, reconciled my reaction and mindfully brought acceptance to past experiences, I'm able to immediately dismiss the fresh attempts to derail my progress and step on, making my and Coco's futures as bright as possible.

While Coco is still part of our family, I can't escape the reminders of our past and I can't change what happened, but I can control my response to those triggered memories.

Over the Christmas break, my mind has naturally looked back over the previous decade and the years that I lost to the accumulation of stress and the resultant mental illness.

I've also spent a lot of time analysing the challenges brought about by the childhood trauma associated with my Congenital Heart Defect and the resultant stoicism and stubbornness.

Without looking back and focusing on my past, I wouldn't have been able to expose the underlying causes of my recent struggles, to rationalise, accept, and even embrace those negative situations and been able to mindfully manage my reaction to the daily triggers that are can never be ignored.

We can't predict the future or tell what's around the next corner and the present is a fleeting moment that passes us by but, even though we can't change the past, we can control how it shapes our future. Not by ignoring it and never looking back but by bringing focus and mindful analysis to sometimes painful situations and more effectively managing our response.

The key to influencing your future lies in how you relate to the demons from your past.

You're Worth It

9th January 2020

Self-priority: never feel guilty about turning yours up once in a while.

It's not weakness, selfish, or embarrassing; it's strength, necessary, and life-changing.

In a world of millions of uncontrollable priorities, be kind to yourself.

You're worth it!

Brighter Flame

9th January 2020

So, you've been diagnosed with a mental illness and you feel scared, confused, shocked, and, due to everything you've been through up to that point, absolutely terrible.

A million new thoughts, questions, and concerns spiral round your already fully occupied mind.

What does the future hold?

How will this be taken at work?

How will my family and friends react?

What can I do?

Why has this happened?

Could I have done anything to prevent it?

Am I to blame?

How will I cope?

Will I be able to cope?

Why am I so weak?

I am such a failure.

All valid questions and concerns that you struggle to answer and just make you feel even worse.

Your sleep hygiene is even more disturbed.

You comfort eat even more.

You don't want to leave the house.

You don't want to leave your bed.

You don't want to feel so alone.

But alone, in your bed, you feel safe. No-one can touch you there, no-one can harm you, no-one can make you feel more dreadful!

You may be prescribed medication to help but the myriad of side effects brings more concerns that cause more damage.

You feel a failure for having to take them but hope they will bring some peace. Your patience is wafer thin, but the medication will take time to have any effect.

You feel trapped, frightened, embarrassed, hopeless, and depressed.

You see others running marathons, when you struggle to run a bath.

You see others climbing mountains, when you struggle to climb the stairs.

You see others enjoying their family, when you struggle to enjoy yourself.

You see others jetting off on holiday, when you struggle to leave your bed.

The medication makes you sleepy but that just brings the nightmares, the flashbacks, the night sweats, the trauma, and you wake up even more exhausted.

How has the diagnosis helped when it just makes everything so real, so challenging, and so final?

You dread the thought of forthcoming medical investigations and reliving your challenges during impending counselling sessions. The fear is paralysing, you feel like nothing could make things worse but dread the things that may help to make things better.

When the physical tests reveal no clues, your fear-filled brain fails to believe and more uncertainty swamps your already flooded mind.

Friends try to help encouraging you to socialise, but that leaves you feeling more of a frump.

Fitness gurus try to increase your exercise, but the sheer enormity of their plans just adds to your fear.

Family are supportive but bring unintended suffocation.

Initiatives are started to encourage group exercise, but the fear of failure and embarrassment triggers lame excuses to explain your non-attendance.

In a binary world that sees everything in black and white, you're either a sloth or a sprinter, a failure or a success, a loser or a champion.

The distance between the place you are and the place the world expects you to be is immense and the expectations to cover the ground in as few steps as possible, impossible.

It's all too black and the white, too dim, out of focus and, from your current position, too far out of reach.

You half-heartedly attend your initial counselling session with great trepidation. A totally alien situation that you feel you don't need, that won't help, and can't provide a means of traversing the chasm that stands between you and better health.

And then your counsellor triggers a flicker of a glimmer of a spark in your mind.

"Imagine you were going on a 500-mile journey, you wouldn't

attempt it one drive, but you'd plan to break it up into more manageable steps. Steps that would reduce the chances of problems with your car, allow you to rest and recover, to take on refreshment and, if necessary, to re-plan your route to account for any setbacks.

In the same way as your journey to better health is a long one, allow it to be broken up into smaller, more manageable and achievable steps.

Steps that would reduce the chances of reoccurrence of your physical health problems, that would give you guilt-free permission to rest, recover, and be refreshed and, by celebration of your progress (no matter how slight), would allow you to cope with any setbacks, to re-plan and continue your journey."

A recovery from any mental illness is daunting. It is challenging and fraught with setbacks and dangers but by introducing a few minutes of focused self-care into your lives each day, the flicker becomes a glimmer that triggers a spark that builds into a flame and hope starts burning brighter.

Small Steps, Gradual Growth, Positive Progress
11th January 2020

When you are battling a mental illness or recovering from a physical injury or illness, it's perfectly natural to feel overwhelmed or daunted when you think about reengaging with a world that may have left you behind.

Reconnecting, emerging from your imposed safety/comfort zone and proving yourself again can feel like massive, impossible, and frightening strides into the unknown.

When your confidence has been destroyed and your reputation damaged, the fear that overpowers your mind and the size of the challenges that lie ahead make standing still feel safer, easier and your only option.

Taking small steps forward, at your pace and in a comfortable secure direction, with friendly support, will change your view.

Small steps reduce the chance of failure, gradually increase your confidence and the impact of any problems that occur can be limited by marking your progress with quiet celebration that builds a buffer to cushion any expected stumbles.

As your self-assurance increases, your steps become more positive, your outlook brighter and the once unreachable strides begin to appear accessible.

Small steps, gradual growth, positive progress …

Keep stepping!

Changed for the Better

18ᵗʰ January 2020

The squirrels at the Squirrel Cafe are taking a well-deserved break from cooking bacon so me and Coco have been trying different routes for our Saturday morning jaunt.

A beautiful day for a walk through the dunes and along the beach and the perfect opportunity to reframe a sly attack by my mental illness this morning.

When I woke up, the little shit tried to pounce on the slightly negative thoughts that were whirring through my mind.

"You'll never feel the highs you felt in 2018. Look what you've lost. Look what I've taken from you," it said.

And then as me and Coco walked along the side of the train track, the recognition and rationalisation.

I completely agree with everything my mental illness said.

It's no surprise to me what I've lost or what has been taken from me, and I'm at peace with those losses.

And, because I've reached a higher plateau, equivalent highs are harder to achieve, and I'm far happier in my current loftier position.

So, I thanked my mental illness for giving me the opportunities it has given me. Without its interference, I would never have had the drive to experience the highs from the lows it had subjected me too.

It's changed me for the better, even though it wasn't very happy with my reaction this morning!

Self-Care

27th January 2020

Self-care: the gift you can give yourself that will benefit others!

Help one person at a time and start by helping you!

YNWA!

"Stereotypes are there to be broken,
Traditions started,
Rules written,
Moulds smashed,
Limits tested,
Boundaries pushed,
Barriers demolished,
Perceptions overlooked,
Lies exposed,
Promises kept,
Problems solved,
Wrongs righted,
Difficulties overcome,
Relationships nurtured,
Care given,
Love shared.

The world may see you through its broken,
blinkered and prejudiced eyes but you will
stand proud, unique, strong and true. For
you are there to be you, no matter your
colour, creed, beliefs, needs or status!

Hey you, be you!"

February 2020

Stepping Stones

9th February 2020

Stepping stones are used to cross rivers and streams and, for me, they represent, as was mentioned at a recent Time to Talk session, a journey through and across the constant flow of the torrent of mental illness.

The stones are relentlessly battered by the river's current, yet they stand firm and allow progress to those willing to take responsibility for their own steps, on their path to recovery, and allow them access to a different view on the opposite bank.

The first step is always the most difficult.

The fear of stepping into the unknown and the threat of being swept away by unexpected undercurrents are real.

After taking that first step, there is period of stabilisation as you become accustomed to your new surroundings, and you start to gauge the severity of the challenges that lie ahead.

You may have glimpsed a view of your destination but, as you expose yourself more to the ravages of the water flow, your nervousness increases and the need for rest and stability after each step becomes more important.

Bravely you take the next step, you rest, you stabilise, and you recover before stepping further on.

As you progress to the halfway point of the river, the middle stone, which is subjected to the greatest force of water, wobbles and your balance and confidence is tested. Before you started your crossing, you were forewarned of this possibility and this allows you to take a step backwards, if necessary, and rest on previous successes.

After a period of recovery, you feel able to face the uncertainty of the unstable stone that lies ahead.

You step on to the unsteady rock again. Refreshed you have the strength to balance for enough time to allow you to pass the halfway point. With safety, calm, and peace in sight and fear reducing, you confidently step on to reach your goal.

You leap from the final stone on to the lush, firm, welcoming embankment and ground your feet.

Turning to face your vanquished foe, realising the anxiety that you have conquered and recognising the power of your mind, both negatively and positively, you celebrate and resolve to build on the awareness gleaned from your trials, tribulations, triumphs and techniques.

Knowing that future rivers will need crossing and accepting that their negative forces will again foster fear, you vow to proactively recognise the challenges ahead, to take that first step and to confidently traverse each crossing with greater resilience and self-assurance.

Stepping stones, spanning the gap between anxiety and tranquillity.

"A true act of selflessness is to sacrifice something for someone even though you know they will never see it!"

"Don't spend all your time looking for someone's 'typos' that you fail to see their 'beautiful composition'."

Coco

In December 2012, our dog of seven years, Kizzy, passed away. Like our two dogs before her, Kizzy had been a massive support to me by encouraging me to exercise and regain my confidence after my catheter ablation in 2004.

Kizzy came into our lives in November 2005, a year after my ablation. By that time, my heart was more stable, and I was ready to push myself and rebuild my fitness. Over the next five years, we would walk for miles and miles and by 2009 my stamina, fitness, and health were at their best levels in my life.

When I was signed off with stress in 2012, Kizzy was my psychological support.

She would sit with me, bring calm into my life, and cajole me to continue to exercise. Soon after I returned to work, Kizzy started to struggle and was diagnosed with cancer in the October of that year.

Looking back and she was probably struggling with her illness while I was struggling with stress, but she hid her problems to concentrate on me. I've never met a dog that was as caring and as loving as Kizzy.

Losing Kizzy left a massive hole in my life, I continued to exercise but it just wasn't the same. I missed our walks and opportunity to offload with my soul mate, especially considering that, even though I was back at work, the stress levels had increased after she had died.

Eventually, I decided to try and find another dog. I searched the rescue centres but none of them fitted my requirements.

In June 2013, I found a dog at the local RSPCA centre but when we visited the centre to meet the dog, it had already been rehomed. We looked at the other dogs but none of them were suitable.

Before we left, we decided to give this scruffy cross-terrier a chance and she was brought out in the paddock.

She immediately hit it off with my youngest son and seemed the best of a bad bunch.

Looking back and I believe that she put on a show that day to try and convince me to take her to her forever home.

I wasn't totally convinced.

We were the first people to look at her in the eight months she'd been in the centre. The RSPCA staff didn't have a great deal of information about her history. She didn't seem a suitable replacement for Kizzy. We struggled to connect.

After a second visit, I decided to give her a chance and on the 15th of July 2013, Coco came to her new home. Little did I know at the time, but she would not only replace Kizzy but, given Coco's undiscovered challenges, she'd surpass her.

Less than a month after Coco came home, my heart exploded with the most severe palpitations I'd experienced in nine years.

Overnight, all the fitness that I'd build up with Kizzy disappeared and my confidence sank to new lows. Thankfully, Coco had picked up Kizzy's mantle and, unbeknown to me, she'd lead me through the most challenging time of my life and, together, we'd explore the devastating power of anxiety, in both our lives, and discover the enriching strength of mindfulness and reconciliation.

It soon became clear that Coco was different, that things had happened in her formative years that had impacted her mentally.

During the first few months, she started to reveal the initial extent of her challenges, but it would take years to peel back the damage and begin to see the full extent of her mental illness.

She'd crave attention but would struggle to accept kindness. A simple stroke would set her on edge, and she'd give out an early warning growly purr when it became too much, before snapping if the sign wasn't recognised. If we moved our feet too quickly when she lay on the floor, she'd jump and react aggressively.

We assumed that she had been mistreated when she was a puppy. Play fights, that should have been part of her growing up, became exercises of caution as she filled her mouth with my arm, carefully ensuring that she didn't bite down on my skin.

The warden at the RSPCA had told us about the time that a Husky had jumped into Coco's pen and how Coco had clinically defended herself by piercing the Husky's nose.

But, despite all these challenges, when Coco felt secure enough to show love it was all-encompassing, deep-rooted, and incredibly powerful.

During my years of palpitations, she would cajole me to continue to exercise and not vegetate on the sofa. She would be patient and understanding when I needed to rest. She would listen when I needed to offload. She would always be by my side when I needed a friend.

Without her support, my fitness levels would have dropped through the floor. Without her encouragement, my recovery would have been even more challenging and protracted. Without her kindness, friendship, and counselling, I would have lost faith in so many things.

She kept me going, she kept me sane, she kept me alive. All that while she battled her own internal, invisible, and ingrained impediments.

The further we walked, the closer we came. The more we discovered about her past, the greater the bond for our future.

In 2014, a couple of months after I suffered two of the worst bouts of palpitations in my life, I decided to take on a challenge and walk 3,000 in a year, an average of seven and a half miles a day.

Coco walked with me for most of those miles and accompanied me over the finish line, after a twenty-seven-mile walk in aid of the

British Heart Foundation.

As I discovered during my recovery, that challenge was counter-productive to my health in that it was forced exercise which didn't allow my body to rest and recover and, in hindsight, made my undiagnosed mental illness worse.

Following my diagnosis of mental illness and cardiology check-up, I realised that I needed to relax during exercise, not push myself too hard and give my body time to recover.

During the first few months of recovery, Coco played a major part in rebuilding my confidence and that undoubtedly allowed my recovery to gather pace.

In October 2017 though, Coco's life was turned upside down by an incident that changed how we'd exercise together and could have cost her life, the similarities to my struggles were palpable.

When on a short evening walk, a dog tried to attack Coco.

Immediately, Coco's instinctive defensive traits kicked in and she overpowered the other dog, even though it was 50% bigger than her, and pinned it to the ground with her teeth imbedded in its ear and her jaw clamped shut.

The initial impact had knocked me off my feet and when I regained my composure, I manage to prize Coco's mouth open and release the other dog's ear.

After carrying Coco to a safe distance, the other owner took their dog home and, as the other owner was at fault, I thought that would be the end of the incident.

Two weeks later I returned home, after visiting a friend from Church, to find two Police Officers in my living room.

After receiving their vet's bill, the other owner had decided to report the incident to the Police and instigate a Civil Complaint against me and Coco.

After explaining the incident from my perspective, I hoped that the complaint would be dropped but in February 2018 I was ordered to attend the Magistrates Court to hear whether Coco would be put under a life-long Control Order or be put to sleep by a Destruction Order.

Before the Court appearance, I had agreed with the Police Solicitor that I would abide by the Control Order if the Destruction Order was disregarded and, thankfully, the Judge agreed that this punishment was sufficient.

From that moment on, Coco would be muzzled when on her walks, on a fixed-length lead and wearing a full-body harness to prevent her from breaking free.

The first time I put Coco's muzzle on, I was filled with trepidation.

How would a nervous dog deal with being defenceless?

Would she refuse to walk outside, or would she take it all in her stride?

As I had put my trust in her when I was struggling with disabling palpitations, she trusted me to protect her from any future incidents. She bravely stepped on and we continued to enjoy our walks, albeit a little differently, and our bond became even stronger as we stepped on together.

I can't thank Coco enough for the support she gave me, from the day she was rescued and came to her new forever home, through the years of challenges that neither of us understood and onto her new restrained future.

The only way I can repay her is to be by her side and protect her in any way that I can.

The way she adapted to the constraints imposed on her by the Control Order is a massive inspiration to me, her bravery allowed me to continue to step on in my recovery.

I rescued her and she rescued me.

"X is the strongest letter in the alphabet ... a well-timed, heartfelt, and genuine one can lift a person off the floor and on to cloud 9!"

"Being misunderstood by someone who doesn't have a clue, validates your ways and verifies your being!"

The Final Chapter?

During my recovery, I've written several "final" chapters and during my challenges I had numerous false dawns when I thought I'd turned a corner only to hit another brick wall that knocked me back, massively.

Only now, as I glimpse a brighter future, have I realised that maybe there never will be a final chapter and that a battle with mental illness is an ongoing, life-long, and constant challenge. A challenge to recognise triggers that life constantly puts in my way, to understand their effects, and rationalise my reaction.

This realisation allows me to reduce the levels of monitoring and, instead, focus on continuing to connect with the world that has moved on, and in many ways has left me behind.

While the act of reconnection, from a world I once thrived in, used to trigger bitterness, frustration, anger, and resentment, now that my confidence has been rebuilt, through counselling, visualisation, mindfulness, and forgiveness, I'm able to reframe those negative traits to my advantage and step on.

As demonstrated by my narrative writing, I've learnt an incredible amount about my mental illness and how to manage its impact.

The journey has been both challenging and enlightening in equal measures but given these lessons and with the help of many people, some that I've known for years and others that have crossed my path more recently, I feel more rounded and more able to, hopefully, deal with any future encounters with my invisible assailant.

When the Occupational Health Doctor diagnosed my mental illness, I never expected how that diagnoses would change my life in such a profound way and, looking back, how it would make me stronger and more aware of life's challenges. How it would bring confidence that has allowed me to pass on my experiences to others and help to change the culture at work that was so instrumental in my demise.

In February 2019, as part of the cultural changes, we started monthly Time to Talk sessions at work. Each session brought together several colleagues to share experiences of mental illness, to pass on techniques to improve well-being and offer support to those who were at different stages of their journey.

As part of the ongoing cultural change being implemented in my workplace, several colleagues have qualified to be frontline Mental Health First Aiders, line managers have been trained in Mental Health Awareness and, most importantly, the changes are being driven by the board of executives.

A year after starting the Time to Talk sessions, after sharing recent triggers that had threatened to reignite my mental illness, the term "self-management" was mentioned during a Time to Talk session and, the morning after, I realised that phase summed up my progress and the steps I had taken in the thirty months since my diagnosis.

Given the circumstances of my situation, and the internal nature of my physical struggles, it soon became apparent that I would need to manage and drive a lot of the changes myself, with the help and support of family, friends, and, of course, Coco.

When my counsellor advised me to challenge my anxiety and see the reality, following my positive cardiology report, he gave me the impetus and authority to take control of my destiny and, unlike my two heart operations, take personal responsibility to make changes that would reduce and then eventually eradicate the effects of my mental illness.

This authority allowed me to uncover a myriad of discoveries, techniques, and implement life changes that would place me in a more stable position both physically and psychologically.

During my journey, I've connected with several people through various Facebook groups who've become valued online friends and provided a massive amount of support and encouragement. I've also been introduced to various specialists including Dr Gabor Maté whose books and podcasts revolutionised my views on mental illness and brought a different perspective on the socially accepted approach to deal with life's challenges.

One of the most important revelations is the acceptance of negativity which flies in the face of the trendy outlook that total positivity is the only way to live your life and thoughts of negativity should be forbidden.

To go through life expecting that nothing will go wrong is like a boxer getting into the ring without any training or preparation and then being knocked out by the first negative blow. A World Champion Boxer, on the other hand, expects to be hit from all angles, with various intensities and for the entire length of the bout. To minimise the impacts, the boxer will spend hours sparring with opponents to build up resilience and prepare their body to withstand the undesirable punishment.

The same applies to how we handle life's unavoidable challenges.

By accepting that difficult times will occur in our lives, we give ourselves the authority to proactively prepare for the fallout that is associated with those moments.

In the same way that the boxer is ready for the onslaught and able to endure the consequences, by recognising that bad times will transpire, we can reduce the possibility of being floored by knock-out blows.

This doesn't mean that we should be pessimistic about life and search out damaging situations. Life by its very nature will always throw challenges in our path and, instead of hiding the negativity behind false positivity and suffering the consequences, being aware will enable us to take the knocks, to ride out the surges and continue to live our lives to their full extent.

The start of the 2020 was full of negative triggers, both personally, nationally, and internationally.

There were times when my anxiety threatened to re-ignite but the increased knowledge of the impact and dangers of my mental illness allowed me to apply the six Rs to each situation and dampen the effects of the negativity.

Reassess, Recognise, Rationalise, React, Rest, and Recover.

Reassess life's challenges and proactively anticipate unexpected situations.

Recognise the triggers and their potential to increase your levels of anxiety.

Rationalise your thoughts and challenge the authenticity of your fears.

React with acceptance and kindness instead of tension and fear.

Rest when necessary to prevent damaging flare ups of psychological problems.

Recover until you feel ready to step on.

By applying the six Rs, I've discovered that I've developed a new outlook on life.

I've always been laid back but, because of the challenges associated with my Congenital Heart Defect, my apparent carefree approach to life was tainted by stoicism and excessive selflessness. These traits enabled me to survive many of the health scares that I've encountered but I now realise that they have been detrimental to my mental health.

The increased awareness of the power of poor mental health and the steps I've taken to recover from my challenges has uncovered new traits which before would have been alien to me. I still have the same laid-back personality and continue to be selfless but now I instinctively realise that I need to employ self-care to protect myself from being taken advantage of by other people and to ensure that my health doesn't suffer.

One quote from Dr Gabor Maté's book "When the Body Says No: The Cost of Hidden Stress" sums this approach up.

"If a refusal (to take on extra responsibility) saddles you with guilt, while consent leaves resentment in its wake, opt for the guilt."

In this quote, Dr Maté is not suggesting we become totally selfish but through the use of the six Rs we become more aware of the effects of not being able to say "no" and being taken for granted. To push back, for our own sake.

Guilt is a temporary emotion that passes as situations change but, as I've found, resentment burrows deeper, is difficult to expose and address and, as Dr Maté eloquently and succinctly states –

"Resentment is soul suicide."

"Spontaneity is the surprise of life ... it's ok to wonder and ponder but better to guess and press!"

"Have you got a friend who you care deeply about but, for whatever reason, haven't been in touch with for a period of time? A simple text, email or smile could make all the difference!"

The Biggest Test

As I finished the previous chapter, it soon became apparent that it wouldn't be the final chapter of this book. In the first few months of 2020, a series of events occurred on a personal, national, and international level that provided an abundance of triggers for my mental illness.

- Before the last chorus of Auld Lang Syne had even died down, American forces had killed a high-ranking Officer in the Iranian army, sparking fears of all-out war breaking out in the Middle East.

- Comments I'd made to try to help people on a Congenital Heart Defect Facebook page were rebuffed and rebuked by a fellow patient.

- Several members of my Church family had sadly passed away.

- Flashbacks and phantom palpitations after hearing about someone else's struggles with Supra Ventricular Tachycardia and watching similar scenes on Casualty.

- Recognising, one morning, that my mental illness was laughing at me. Telling me what it had taken from me and what I had lost. Realisation of the friendships and relationships that have been damaged and the struggles to reconnect.

- Struggling with Red January and how I felt it had been "hijacked" as an exercise competition which reduced the impact of this great initiative and possibly caused greater anxiety and suffering to those who couldn't physically complete, because of their psychological issues.

- Society's focus on Blue Monday which belittles the constant everyday struggle with mental illness and brings flippancy to words such as "anxiety", "depression", and "OCD". This reduces their impact and has a major destabilising effect on those who live with the constant, unrelenting, intense damage caused by these misunderstood disorders.

- Supporting my wife through her stepfather's illness, including long periods sat at his bedside during his last days.

But given my progress and discoveries, and as I was fully aware of how devastatingly powerful anxiety can be, I was more able to recognise the triggers.

Once the triggers were recognised, I could take steps to identify the causes, to rationalise my response, to choose a more considered reaction, to ask for help, if required, and, instead of stoically and naively forcing myself on (as I've done all my life), give myself permission to rest, recover, and render the triggers impotent.

The following techniques and processes, that I've discovered during my recovery from mental illness, and outlined in this book, allowed me to mitigate the fallout from the situations and maintain a degree of control -

- Forgiveness; making peace with my past to lighten my future.
- Gratitude; noticing and being thankful for the little but important things in my life.
- Acceptance; bringing kindness and sensitivity to my challenges.
- Habit changing; consciously altering my ingrained, defensive reactions to life's situations. No longer stoically and naively forcing myself on.
- Dietary changes; being more aware of what I was eating.
- Focused relaxation; introducing mindfulness and breathing techniques into my life.

- Writing; offloading my concerns and worries in a journal.
- Time offline; spending time with a brew and a friend.
- Sleep hygiene; taking steps to improve the quality of my sleep.
- And most importantly, taking small steps, reducing the chance of failure, and celebrating every little success, even if it was something I used to do with ease before my struggles.

But behind all these triggers, silently, quietly, and ominously, a major threat was developing on the other side of the world.

At the end of December 2019, a novel coronavirus had emerged in central China and, despite suspension of international travel and total lockdown at the epicentre, the virus quickly spread to Iran, Italy, France, and Spain before the first cases slowly started to develop in the United Kingdom.

At first it appeared that there was a possibility that the virus could be contained, and the impact would be minimised but at the end of March, it became clear that major changes to normal life would be necessary to reduce the reach of the virus and a lockdown was instigated by the Government across the whole country.

Anxiety levels shot up as people emptied the shelves of essential items, businesses were closed, families were unable to meet, people were instructed to stay in their homes and work from home if possible. The Government took steps to minimise the impact by announcing grants for businesses and money to furlough staff to prevent mass redundancies.

Uncertainty for the future gripped everyone, nobody knew what the future would look like, the National Health Service was in danger of being overwhelmed and the death rates that started off low, grew at an alarming rate. The news was full of grim statistics and predications.

The biggest threat to physical and mental health for decades loomed over the world and a sense of hopelessness and anxiety swept across the globe.

Like everyone, I became very concerned with this world crisis. But, as I've recognised from my previous challenges, I refused to be affected by something that is far more dangerous, the effects of fear itself.

Given my heart defects and knowing how my heart had reacted in the past to viruses, I realised that I was more vulnerable to the outbreak. However, the chances of contracting the virus were far less than the damage that anxiety had caused in the past.

So, as well as taking precautions to protect myself, my family, and my community, e.g. improved hand hygiene, trying not to touch my face, and social distancing, I recognised how important it was to keep an eye on my anxiety levels.

All four precautions reduce the chances of infection but the last one is the most powerful.

Being adaptive to situations, accepting things that I can't change and changing the things I can, helped to reduce my anxiety levels which, in turn, boosted my immune system.

Taking responsibility for my actions, as no one else can do what I need to do, while I hoped that others would take equal responsibility to protect themselves and this would help flatten the curve for the benefit of everyone.

I know that if this happened in 2017, when fear and anxiety were in full control of my life, the consequences would have been disastrous. But now I'm more in control of the fear and anxiety.

I'd retrained my brain to be more rational and less reactionary (yes, it is possible to make your brain think differently), my heart was beating like a dream and my immune system felt stronger. I'd started being proactively adaptive in finding solutions to problems and realised again the importance of the simple breathing technique that I'd been using since 2017.

Anxiety loves uncertainty, it's its life blood and, for obvious reasons, it was thriving on a massive scale as the virus continued to spread.

For me, and many others, the worst time for uncertainty is in the early hours of the morning.

Waking up in the middle of the night triggers your brain into overdrive and the uncertainty flares up weird and outrageous thoughts that wouldn't be entertained during the day.

With your mind whirring uncontrollably, sleep at best is fleeting and at worst impossible.

But there is hope.

I've been practicing mindfulness for two and a half years but, until now, I didn't fully appreciate the importance and power of a simple breathing technique and the certainty it will bring to an uncertain situation.

To put it plainly, when you are thinking, you must be breathing, and this realisation brings the hope for a change.

By switching your mind's focus to your breathing and concentrating on taking gentle slow breaths, your thoughts are hushed, and your breath's certainty means sleep is no longer an impossible dream.

By breathing in acceptance and kindness to the situation, while breathing out tension and fear, you begin to bring rationalisation to your thoughts and calm to your anxious mind.

Instead of fight or flight hormones being released, putting your body on high alert, the soothing breaths induce the calmer "tend and be-friend" reaction. It feels like your Vagus Nerve is gently caressing your internal organs, your brain recognises their signals and starts to settle.

It's important during anxious times to be aware of the power of a simple breath and to harness that power for the good of your mental and physical health.

Start to practice focusing on your breathing, it takes time and patience but, trust me, even in times of great uncertainty, its life changing power is certain.

While facing the trials of the first three months of 2020, I've got to know two parts of my brain a lot better.

Let me call them Reactionary Reg and Conscious Colin.

When my life was pre-occupied with mental health challenges, Reactionary Reg was in charge and my brain had no time or space for Conscious Colin.

The problem with Reactionary Reg is that he can't think for himself and instead relies on past experiences and, as his name suggests, previous reactions. Reg is swayed by social media posts, over reactions, and ignorant responses. Every decision Reg makes, without any input from Colin, pushes you further down into the depths of despair, reducing Colin's influence even more.

And with Colin out of the picture, Reg can run riot.

The challenge is to find a way to reduce Reg's control and reinvigorate Colin's conscious guidance.

The problem is, how do you tell your brain to think differently? After all, your brain controls your thoughts, doesn't it?

Around the middle of January, when the Reg was trying to reinvigorate past experiences of anxiety, I recognised his attempts and looked for ways to counter the attack.

Thankfully, unlike in 2017, I'd spent two and a half years mindfully rebuilding my confidence and, because of that, Conscious Colin was able to step in and intervene.

And then it hit me. Even though Reg couldn't think for himself, Colin could think for him, and he could sway Reg's reaction with fact and reality-based evidence.

It wasn't a case of telling my brain to think differently, it was a case of consciously empowering Colin to alter Reg's ingrained, instinctive, and mindless reaction.

So that's what I did and with help from breathing and mindfulness techniques, Colin recognised and rationalised each situation, bringing reality to the fore, reframing my response, authorising time to rest, recover, and encouraging Reg to rethink his reaction.

With Colin back in charge, instead of Reg relying on previous negative experiences, they are now both working in harmony. Reg is being re-educated which allows difficult situations, although very challenging, to be addressed in a conscious, aware, and balanced way.

And, believe it or not, it is possible to teach your brain to think differently and to change entrenched reactions, like instinctively touching your face, for better self-care.

By getting in touch with your Conscious Colin, you can bring more positivity to Reg's reactions.

Looking after yourself is your greatest power and doesn't rely on anyone else's decision.

During the battle with the virus, and when dealing with the challenges of lockdown, there has never been a more important time to talk about anxiety, and more specifically how excessive levels can trigger pre-existing physical conditions or manifest into new physical symptoms and reactions.

There are various levels of anxiety, ranging from everyday challenges to the current world situation.

All levels are equally important to the person living with the anxiety, but the widespread psychological reach of the world pandemic is, for the majority, the first time that they have felt the full force of severe anxiety and the associated life or death consequences.

How this might affect society's future view of mental illness, e.g. reduced stigma and discrimination, is yet to be seen but, more pressingly, what are the immediate threats and what steps can we take to address and lessen their impact?

As mentioned previously, there are three instances from my battles with excessive levels of anxiety that instantly spring to mind. All of them in different circumstances but all with one thing in common, the physical symptoms that were triggered were not instigated by a physical infection but caused by my mental illness.

In 2012, after months of stress and anxiety, every morning I would cough and retch for hours before work. I showed all the symptoms of having a virus but, after being signed off sick for six weeks and taking time to rest, the coughing stopped.

In 2013, during the implementation of a project at work, my heart went into severe palpitations while I was sat at my desk. In previous years, this would have been the early warning sign of a bug, but after recognising and removing the reason for the trigger, my heart instantly reverted to a normal sinus rhythm.

In 2014, a day after the dentist cut my gum while preparing a filling, my heart burst into a debilitating arrhythmia which lasted for thirty-six hours. It had all the hallmarks of an infection that could have incapacitated me for weeks, but when my heart miraculously reset itself, my recovery was almost instant.

These situations illustrate the importance of preventing the build of excessive levels of anxiety and the immense value in initiating proactive steps at the earliest opportunity to diminish the power and reach of psychological issues.

When we are stressed and anxious, our body reacts to the impending danger by releasing hormones to allow us to deal with the situation and decide whether we need to fight the assailant or take flight from the threat.

But when we are stressed and anxious over a long period of time, our body isn't designed to deal with the continuous flow of adrenaline.

When faced with this onslaught, our immune system becomes confused leading to greater susceptibility to viruses, bugs, and other ailments. And, most significantly, our default reaction to everyday situations is to become tense, angry, bitter, and resentful, exposing us to more stress and anxiety.

It's very easy to allow this situation to quickly spiral out of control, to burrow deeper and cause long-lasting, debilitating, and dangerous repercussions to our mental and physical health.

But there is another way and, given the importance and uncertainty of the global situation with the constant stream of negative news, it was imperative to take steps to try to view things in a different light.

By replacing the ensconced tension and fear with liberating acceptance and kindness, your default reaction can be gradually altered which is particularly important during anxiety-filled times.

The technique I utilised advises a different approach to personal situations, relationships, and encounters with others and is based on understanding, acceptance, kindness, sensitivity, and forgiveness.

This brings a transformed view of everyday occurrences, reducing the possibility of anxiety being triggered, recognising the things that can't be changed, concentrating on things that can be changed and allowing your immune system to be better primed to battle unwanted intruders.

For my heart operations, I relied totally on the skill and experience of the doctors and surgeons. For my battle with mental illness, all the power was in my mind and this technique was the catalyst that started a revolution in my head.

This technique, together with the four Rs outlined below, enables massive changes to be realised –

- Recognise the triggers

- Rationalise your thoughts and reactions

- Allow your mind and body to rest and recover.

As I mentioned, in 2014 I experienced a thirty-six-hour battle with intense palpitations. Every year since, I've marked the anniversary by reliving that battle and, by doing so, prolonging its hold on my life.

This year's anniversary was the same.

For most of the day I was solemn, quiet, and reflective, pondering if I should post on Facebook, continue the cycle and extend the reach of that dark time for another year.

Then came the refocus and the reframing. Then came the realisation that I had the perfect opportunity to break that annual cycle.

So, I did, and instantly my day changed.

Then, when I looked at my Facebook memories, it all fell into place.

With perfect timing, a post by the inspirational Facebook support group Wild Wellness from last year brought validation to my decision and reminded me of the steps I've taken since those difficult days.

The post outlines an approach that goes against the grain of society but, given the situation of a global pandemic, couldn't be more effective and beneficial.

After my perennial wobble, it certainly put me back on the right path and summarised everything that I'd discovered on my journey.

Wild Wellness

Our minds are very powerful – they run our lives, tell our lungs to breathe, give us opportunities to learn, and allow us to function on a semi-permanent auto-pilot for many of our daily tasks.

They can also become prisons, places to be held against our will, serving toxic thoughts.

The answer can't be found by running away; how can you run away from yourself? The answer can only come from "sitting down with yourself and asking what is wrong here".

We need the courage to be spiritually adult and face our distress/worry/anxiety /fear in order to understand where it is coming from. When we know this, we can start to unravel our complex powerful emotions to let these negative states of mind go and never return.

In Buddhist teaching, you can train and control your mind through meditation. There is no religious belief required, only the willingness to engage with an open mind. Our minds are our responsibility along with our happiness or sadness.

So, we do have choices. We stay attached to our distress, emotional pain, and suffering or we use the techniques of meditation and self-reflection to find ways to de-stress.

Anxiety, fear, and worry never affect positive change. They are emotional states which steal away our ability to achieve happiness and inner peace.

How incredible that you are your own vessel to transform your life. You and your own mind are the key to open your prison and fly freely. You already have this ability for happiness inside you. We just need to summon the courage to begin.

Love and light.

A number of positives can emerge from this period of upheaval, uncertainty, and unseen dangers. Reduced pollution, greater love for family and friends, focus and appreciation of the important things in life, and realisation of the fragility of life.

But given the large-scale exposure to a previously unknown, invisible, and unrecognised assailant, the greatest benefit will be increased understanding of the effects of mental illness.

How it disables.

How it isolates.

How it demoralises.

How it escalates.

How it alienates.

How it can be recognised.

How it can be exposed.

How it can be addressed.

How it can be controlled.

How it can be defeated.

How it can transform.

The stigma and discrimination that came from misunderstanding, misinterpretation, and misdiagnosis will be replaced with tolerance and equality. Conversations that were once silenced will be heard. Loneliness will become companionship. Sadness displaced with joy. Hostility conquered by kindness. Distress with de-stress!

An important lesson to us all and the perfect way to live your life going forward.

I hope the contents of this book have given encouragement and guidance for those living with mental illness.

And always remember to take small steps in any way, distance, and direction that you feel able.

Keep stepping to a brighter, more peaceful, more fulfilling, and enlightened future.

ABOUT THE AUTHOR

Mike Owen lives in the North West of England; he is married with two grown up children.

Outside of his work in IT, he enjoys volunteering at his local Church, leading young people through their teenage years through Boys' Brigade and Youth Clubs. Over the last decade, the youth work has encouraged a number of children with their own individual challenges to feel safe and secure in the Church environment.

Throughout Mike's life, his health problems have been purely physical, with two congenital heart defects. However, following his battle with psychological issues, his personal exposure to the destructive power of poor mental health has opened a new view on his vulnerability. This knowledge has helped in supporting friends, colleagues, and young people in his care, who are facing similar challenges.

Mike has rescued four dogs, all of which helped him during difficult situations, his latest dog, Coco, came to her forever home just before Mike's mental illness was exposed and, despite her own mental health issues, Coco was instrumental in Mike's recovery.

Printed in Great Britain
by Amazon